Spiritual L

Thomas H. Ulrich

Spiritual Leadership

A Guide to Focus, Awareness, and Mindfulness

Thomas H. Ulrich
Munich, Germany

ISBN 978-3-030-45431-9   ISBN 978-3-030-45432-6   (eBook)
https://doi.org/10.1007/978-3-030-45432-6

Original German edition published by Springer Gabler, Wiesbaden, Germany

This Springer imprint is published by the registered company Springer Nature Switzerland AG.
The registered company address is: Gewerbestrasse 11, 6330 Cham, Switzerland

For Tim and Jan
и
для О.

Preface

There is a perfection,
deep in the midst of all inadequacy.
There is a silence,
deep in the midst of helplessness.
There is a goal,
deep in the midst of all worldly cares.
…
Let your mind become still,
like a pond in the forest.
Your mind should become clear,
like the water that flows down from the mountains.
Let turbid waters come to rest,
then they will become clear,
and let your wandering thoughts and wishes come to rest.
(Buddha)

To make it clear from the beginning: this book is not a religious book

This book is about working on an aspect of Leadership that is, at the same time, the easiest and the most challenging one: on yourself. To be more precisely: on your Self. It is about building a bridge between classical, rather rational Leadership theories, and Leadership models of Authentic Leadership, via philosophy, Awareness and Mindfulness in various areas of our life, up to meditative practice, developing from them a concept of Spiritual Leadership, based on Focus and Centricity on various levels, to reach the core of inner

Centricity. Each chapter comprises practical exercises on Focus, Awareness and Mindfulness as guidance towards Centricity.

Concerning the Use of Wording in This Book

I decided to talk about myself and about my own experience in this book, and to address you as a reader directly this book, as this book is about very personal issues, about issues that come out of yourself, and refer to your Self. It is about You! When only a male form of a wording is used in the book, then it is only for the sake of simplicity and to keep the flow of text and reading, as of course this book refers equally to both male and female readers without any difference.

Why is it worth to talk about and work on "Spiritual Leadership"? In Management Theories, we constantly hear about buzzwords like Operational Excellence, Customer Centricity, Agility, VUCA, etc. However, modern ways of Leadership also take other issues into their Focus, beyond the mere operational Management. For successful and powerful Leadership, a Leader should be aware of things that lie beyond that operational surface. I firmly believe in a deeper truth, a truth that lies in the core, in the Centre of our Personality, and that has an effect on the key elements of successful and powerful Leadership.

It is about understanding the influence and effect of being focused and centred. It is about working yourself through various levels of Acting, Personality and Spirit. In short: it is about working on Awareness and Mindfulness towards a spiritual core of inner Centricity. In that sense, spiritual does not (necessarily) mean religious. However, you may find for yourself such a spiritual core and inner Centricity in your religion. I am convinced: this is by far not the only way to experience inner Centricity as an effective or even powerful source, a source that can lead you to effective Leadership impact, to Spiritual Leadership.

This book describes various ways and approaches on different levels which can open a way to Spiritual Leadership, based on inner Centricity.

Munich, Germany   Thomas H. Ulrich
March 1, 2020

Acknowledgements

I truly thank everybody from the bottom of my heart who supported me and contributed so that this book finally came into existence.

In particular, I would like to express special acknowledgements to:

Mr Philip Botha of the consultant agency Axialent, who gave me the initial trigger for my recognition and understanding of Centricity, which finally led to this book, by wisely guiding us—a team of Bosch Group managers—through a Leadership retreat on Authentic Leadership.

My family for all their support throughout my personal journey of life, from which many aspects and personal experience made it into this book, and for supporting me during the creation of this book on many evenings and weekends, for giving me the freedom and positive feedback.

A valuable person for completing myself with a kind and open heart, с тобой я совершенный.

Contents

About the Author

The Author T. H. Ulrich (photo: Özgür Ölçer **2016**, with kind authorization of Özgür **Ölçer)**

Thomas H. Ulrich graduated as a physicist from the Justus Maximilians Universität in Würzburg (Diploma) and the Université Joseph Fourier Grenoble (Maîtrise de Physique). Starting his business career in 1994, he worked as Patent Engineer and subsequently as German Patent Attorney and European Patent Attorney with the patent departments of Deutsche Telekom (T-Mobile) and Siemens as well as with DaimlerChrysler and EADS.

In 2004, he started his Leadership career as Head of Intellectual Property with multimedia semiconductor company Micronas and subsequently as Senior Vice President and Head of Intellectual Property with printing press manufacturer manroland (formerly MAN Roland Druckmaschinen). Today his function is Vice President and Corporate Patent Counsel at BSH Hausgeräte Group (formerly BSH Bosch und Siemens Hausgeräte Group) within the Bosch Group.

1

About This Book

This book fist came into existence in German language, and after its publication, I am now revising it and translating it into English language for this subsequent publication, doing so besides my job as a Leader and Manager, on many evenings and weekends. So dear reader I hope you may forgive any shortcomings that you may encounter in this book.

For many of us, life feels like a permanent rush (Fig. 1.1). Myself, as many of us, I lead what has become "a normal academic life". Like many of us, I spent a lot of time to follow many "important" tasks in life: a job that keeps us busy tracking and running behind KPIs, milestones and budget forecasts, in order to meet the annual targets and annual business plan. Besides that, I was busy throughout my whole life with many studies and nonprofessional activities:

Studying physics at universities in Germany and France, and then studying all aspects of law on Intellectual Property (patents, trademark rights, design rights...) besides my jobs. In addition to that, doing sports (basketball, Tae Kwon Do, Aikido, Karate, Iaido, Kickboxing, Fitness practicing dancing and quite some more). In addition, even more studying, reading literature about topics from philosophy and Asian culture to Management and Leadership, learning and practicing photography, and living my passion of learning foreign languages, ending up—besides my mother language German—speaking English, French, and Spanish, and even some basic Chinese, Turkish, and Russian.

Still there was always this—rather subconscious—feeling: something is missing.

After quite some years of study of sciences, law, Leadership styles, and Leadership methods, as well as the aforementioned nonprofessional "arts," I experienced, during a retreat event on Authentic Leadership, a sudden

T. H. Ulrich, *Spiritual Leadership*, https://doi.org/10.1007/978-3-030-45432-6_1

Fig. 1.1 Rush(ing) in India (source: own photo)

moment of understanding. To be more exactly, it was rather a moment of remembering something that had already been there, like little pieces laid out here and there in front of me, but until that moment I just was not able to fit them together to the complete picture:

It is all about Centricity.

I became aware that I already had experienced a glimpse of this understanding several times before. However, for long time I was not able to understand the full scope of it. When I became aware of the full, complete picture, something had changed inside myself, inside my Self: I started my way, my journey to focus consciously focus on Centricity (Fig. 1.2).

Zen Buddhism describes the experience of "Satori," literally translated "understanding." Maybe my personal experience was something like a tiny bit of such a Satori experience; however, I would not use such a big word to describe it. In any case, it is a very special experience when suddenly "the fog is clearing up" and you can see what is laid out in front of you, what had been there already for a long time.

To express it very clearly: I do not see myself as a perfect Leader or a perfect person. Me too, I am just as human being, like all of us, with my own, personal strengths and my own, personal weaknesses. I admit to you very openly,

Fig. 1.2 A symbolic depiction of Centricity (source: http://www.pixabay.com, created by: Pezibear)

dear reader: myself I am still learning and practicing (and struggling with it), if possible every single day. Because it is a lifelong journey.

I nevertheless would like to share with you what I have learnt so far in the 50 years of my past life, from studies of different sciences, arts, cultures, philosophies, literature, etc. and simply from life itself, in all its varieties that our world provides for us, that may appear so different from each other, but that all have a common core. Because—in the end—we are all human beings.

I am especially writing this book for my sons, to convey to them some of the main experiences and learnings that I have collected throughout my past life, in order to give them an inspiration for their own lives. If some more people should find interest in reading this book, I would be more than happy.

2

The Scientific Background: Centricity in Physics

I would like to start with one of the most fascinating phenomena that I encountered during my studies of Physics: the gyro.

When you have the possibility, then I recommend you to try the following experiment yourself, or at least watch some videos on the well-known internet platforms or online encyclopedia (e.g., Wikipedia 2018): the precession of a gyro under the influence of the gravitational field of the earth. Those who would like to learn more about the relevant scientific background in Physics, I recommend standard books of physics that deal with classical mechanics (as German books, I recommend "Gerthsen Physik", Meschede 2015 or "Goldstein"—Klassische Mechanik, Goldstein et al. 2006).

This is what happens:

When the axis, the Center of the gyro, is not aligned with the gravitational field of the earth, i.e., when the axis of the gyro is not upright, then the axis of the gyro starts "tumbling" around a virtual vertical line, around a virtual Center. This tumbling movement is called precession and is depicted in Fig. 2.1 and schematically visualized in Fig. 2.2.

Only when the axis of the gyro is upright, the spinning gyro stands still, without any tumbling movement. The mass of the gyro wheel is spinning fast around the axis of the gyro, around his Center; however, the gyro itself stands still, upright, and centered, as depicted in Fig. 2.3 and schematically visualized in Fig. 2.4.

© The Editor(s) (if applicable) and The Author(s), under exclusive licence to
Springer Nature Switzerland AG 2020
T. H. Ulrich, *Spiritual Leadership*, https://doi.org/10.1007/978-3-030-45432-6_2

Fig. 2.1 Precession movement of a gyro (source: www.pixabay.com, created by Stevebidmead, amended)

What is also interesting in that phenomenon is, even when the axis of the tumbling gyro is tilted and non-centered, the gyro however does not fall down as long as it is still spinning fast enough, as long as it is moving fast enough, and has enough energy. It is tumbling; however, it is not yet falling. It is tumbling and wasting energy on its tumbling movement, because it is not centered; however, it is still able to keep up this tumbling movement around the virtual center, as long as it still has enough remaining energy. Only when the remaining inner kinetic energy gets too low, it falls down, breaks down.

Does that remind you of something? Of something that you have experienced yourself in your own life? How often do you feel like a gyro that is tumbling, but not (yet) falling? You are moving and wasting energy while tumbling around? Does that sound familiar to you?

Here is where Centricity comes into play.

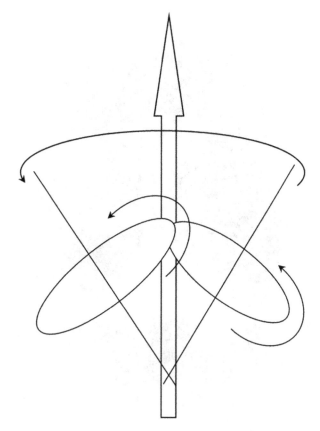

Fig. 2.2 Precession movement of a gyro—schematic visualization (source: own drawing)

Conclusion for Your Leadership

The phenomena of "Centricity" are not something artificial or theoretical, nor are they something new. They are something very real, something that we can perceive nature and that is known to humankind from natural sciences since long time. We will learn in the further course of this book that also from various philosophies, ideas and thoughts are known since thousands of years, that reflect "Centricity," especially "inner Centricity," in the way I would like to lay out in this book.

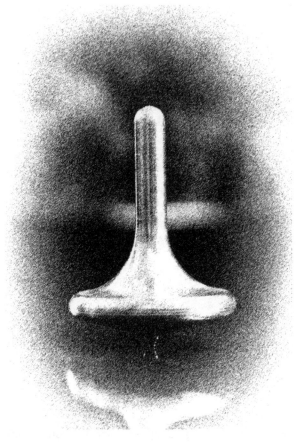

Fig. 2.3 Gyro centered in the gravitational field (source: www.pixabay.com, created by jennyfriedrichs, amended)

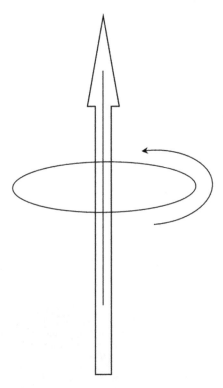

Fig. 2.4 Gyro centered in the gravitational field—schematic visualization (source: own drawing)

References

Goldstein H, Poole CP Jr, Safko JL Sr (2006) Klassische Mechanik. Wiley-VCH Verlag, Weinheim

Meschede D (2015) Gerthsen Physik. Springer, Heidelberg

Wikipedia (2018) Präzession. Wikipedia Die freie Enzyklopädie. https://de.wikipedia.org/wiki/Pr%C3%A4zession. Accessed May 22, 2018

3

The Background in Leadership Theory: Authentic Leadership

As we probably all know, there are multiple Leadership theories and literature about Leadership. From rather classical—and nevertheless quite popular—approaches like depicted in the books of Kenneth Blanchard et al. "The One Minute Manager" (Blanchard et al. 1986; German publication: "Das Minunten-Manager-Buch", Blanchard et al. 2007), or Buckingham and Clifton "Now, Discover Your Strengths" (Buckingham and Coffman 2001; German publication "Entdecken Sie Ihre Stärken jetzt—Das Gallup-Prinzip für individuelle Entwicklung und erfolgreiche Führung", Buckingham and Coffman 2002) up to more "radical" approaches like—again—Buckingham and Clifton "First, Break All The Rules" (Buckingham and Coffman 2005, German publication "Erfolgreiche Führung gegen alle Regeln", Buckingham and Coffman 2012).

For readers who understand German language, I can recommend some more German books on Leadership like Gudrun Heppich "Was wirklich zählt" (Happich 2014) or Sebastian Purps-Pardigol "Führen mit Hirn—Mitarbeiter begeistern und Unternehmenserfolg steigern" (Purps-Partigol 2015) as well as the more "radical" Sprenger "Radikal führen" (Sprenger 2012) and Jotzo "Der Chef den keiner mochte" (Jotzo 2014).

Modern Leadership theories and Leadership literature now tend to take a glance at the "Inside" of the Leader, at what characterizes him as a person and individual. Let us have an exemplary look at publications on Authentic Leadership. There are mainly two basic concepts of Authentic Leadership in literature:

T. H. Ulrich, *Spiritual Leadership*, https://doi.org/10.1007/978-3-030-45432-6_3

1. Extrinsically motivated concepts that chose an intellectual approach in order to develop Authenticity, i.e., by developing an understanding for the own role and for the expectations that others have with respect to that role, in order to consciously work on the character of this role, so to best possible fulfil the expectations with respect to that role.
2. Intrinsically motivated concepts that deal with the approach to find a personal orientation as a Leader, to develop an understanding of who I am as a person, as a personality, and what I stand for, that means to develop out of oneself, out of the own Self, a very personal understanding of Authentic Leadership.

One model of Authentic Leadership—that has become quite popular—is the model of Bill George. To get a deeper understanding of the Authentic Leadership model of Bill George, I would like to recommend you his book "Authentic Leadership—Rediscovering the Secrets to Creating Lasting Value" (George 2003), in which he describes his model of Authentic Leadership as presented here. The model of Bill George is based on the following five dimensions:

Purpose, Values, Heart, Relationships, and Self-Discipline

and on the related development qualities (see Table 3.1).

According to Bill George (2003), there is a strong relationship between the five dimensions and the related development qualities as shown in Fig. 3.1.

According to Bill George, the target status is to be an Authentic Leader. Bill George lays out that this can be achieved by developing awareness and understanding for the five dimensions of the own personality, and by working consciously on the five related development qualities—or the five key areas—that characterize the Authentic Leadership model of Bill George.

Table 3.1 Authentic Leadership dimensions and development qualities by Bill George

Purpose ↔ Passion
Values ↔ Behavior
Heart ↔ Compassion
Relationships ↔ Connectedness
Self-Discipline ↔ Consistency

Source: George (2003), with kind permission of Bill George

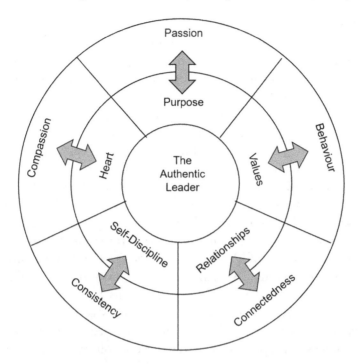

Fig. 3.1 The dimensions and development qualities of Authentic Leadership as of Bill George (Source: "Authentic Leadership" 2003, with kind permission of Bill George)

When the Leader has

– discovered and understood his Values
– that form the basis of his Behavior and personality,
– the Purpose that gives him Passion in his life,
– the important Relationships which he should actively work on by focusing on connecting himself with others,
– etc.,

then he has reached a status in which he can actively use the knowledge about the five dimensions of his personality, which he has discovered for himself, to actively work on the five related development qualities—or key areas—in order to, finally, become an Authentic Leader.

In his later book—written together with Peter Sims—"True North—Discover your Authentic Leadership" (George and Simms 2007), Bill George lays out how to (further) develop oneself as an Authentic Leader by further deepening the relevant key areas of Authentic Leadership.

The Authentic Leadership model of Bill George can be very powerful, as it can help a Leader to understand out of himself, out of his Self, who he is and what he stands for. Based on that understanding, the model can support an authentic self-development of his Leadership, by finding and aligning himself with his personal "North Star," his very personal "True North."

Some time ago, I made my own, very personal experience with Bill George's Authentic Leadership model in our company group (the Bosch Group), by means of Leadership retreats and trainings of our external Coaching provider Axialent, who is specialized on cultural transformation in companies (see Axialent Website 2018). I experienced that it is a great challenge to take Bill George's model seriously and actively work on it. And I am convinced that working on this model of Authentic Leadership can already help many Leaders to improve their Authenticity and with it their impact as a Leader.

However, the notion of "Authenticity" is not so easy to transmit, as some people tend to interpret "Authenticity" as explanation or justification of "Laziness," like Stefan Wachtel points out in his book "Sei nicht authentisch—warum klug manchmal besser ist als echt" (Wachtel 2014). This book is an example of a more intellectual approach to Authenticity, based on a conscious analysis of expectations with respect to your role as a Leader, and—based on these insights—to consciously adapting your appearance and behaviors to these expectations.

Such approach can be very helpful for Leaders who are more analytically and intellectually driven persons, in order to provide them an analytical "planning toolbox" to increase their effectiveness and impact in their Leadership roles.

The difference in "Authenticity" in the approaches of Bill George and Stefan Wachtel is: Stefan Wachtel works out in his book what you can *learn about others* and how you can work on yourself in order to *be perceived authentic* in your *role* and to *actively and consciously create* an *authentic impression*, to *appear authentic*.

George puts his focus on what you can *learn about yourself* and how you can work on yourself in order to *develop an awareness* of *who you are* as an *authentic person*, in order to *truly be authentic.*

Conclusion for Your Leadership

There are multiple Leadership theories and literature about Leadership, of which you can make use in order to further develop yourself as a Leader. It is up to you to find out what fits best for yourself (for your Self-development):

Either an intellectual approach, suitable for persons being predominantly analytically and intellectually driven, providing an analytical "planning toolbox" to increase the effectiveness and impact in the Leadership role, in particular to best meet the extrinsic expectations of others.

Or an intrinsically motivated approach, that helps to find personal orientation as a Leader, to develop an understanding of the own personality, of oneself, of your Self and to understand what you stand for, in order to be truly authentic and centered in yourself.

References

Axialent-Website. https://www.axialent.com/, 2018

Blanchard K et al (1986) The one minute manager. Berkley Trade, New York

Blanchard K et al (2007) Das Minunten-Manager-Buch. Rowohlt, Reinbek bei Hamburg

Buckingham M, Coffman C (2001) Now, discover your strengths. Free Press, New York

Buckingham M, Coffman C (2002) Entdecken Sie Ihre Stärken jetzt – Das Gallup-Prinzip für individuelle Entwicklung und erfolgreiche Führung. Campus; Frankfurt

Buckingham M, Coffman C (2005) First, break all the rules. Pocket Books, London

Buckingham M, Coffman C (2012) Erfolgreiche Führung gegen alle Regeln. Campus, Frankfurt

George B (2003) Authentic leadership – rediscovering the secrets to creating lasting value. Wiley, San Francisco

George B, Simms P (2007) True North – discover your authentic leadership. Wiley, San Francisco

Happich G (2014) Was wirklich zählt. Springer Gabler, Wiesbaden

Jotzo M (2014) Der Chef den keiner mochte. Gabal, Offenbach

Purps-Pardigol S (2015) Führen mit Hirn – Mitarbeiter begeistern und Unternehmenserfolg steigern. Campus, Frankfurt

Sprenger RK (2012) Radikal führen. Campus, Frankfurt

Wachtel S (2014) Sei nicht authentisch – warum klug manchmal besser ist als echt. Plassen, Kulmbach

4

The Concept of Spiritual Leadership and Centricity

First, let us have a look at the definition of "concept":

> Concepts are the fundamental building blocks of our thoughts and beliefs. They play an important role in all aspects of cognition.
>
> …
>
> Cognition is the mental action or process of acquiring knowledge and understanding through thought, experience and the senses. (Wikipedia 2018)

The concept of Spiritual Leadership is focusing on what you can *learn about your Self* and how you can *work on your Self*. The concept of Spiritual Leadership is derived from a wisdom which is frequently said to be originating from oral transmissions of Talmud, or alternatively Lao Tzu (Lǎozǐ 老子) or other historic persons, depending on where you look it up.

This wisdom is:

Watch your thoughts, for they become words.
Watch your words, for they become actions.
Watch your actions, for they become habits.
Watch your habits, for they become character.
Watch your character, for it becomes your destiny.

I chose this wisdom as a basis to develop the concept of Spiritual Leadership as laid out in this book, because it expresses very clearly my personal experience: That there are different levels or layers of our person, our personality, of our Self, that are interconnected, that influence each other, and that are

T. H. Ulrich, *Spiritual Leadership*, https://doi.org/10.1007/978-3-030-45432-6_4

building upon each other. At the Center of it, there is one big thing: It is at the core of us, the core of our Self.

It is about Centricity, and—at the core of it—about inner Centricity.

When Centricity—especially inner Centricity—is there, then our Self becomes very powerful, because everything that defines our Self and makes our Self visible and tangible for others around us naturally falls into place. This naturally leads to true Authenticity.

If Centricity is not there, then our Self and our appearance and impact on others appear artificial, ridiculous.

I will lay out the concept of Spiritual Leadership in detail in the following chapters, describing my own experience and personal understanding, which I have discovered via a journey that took many years, a learning journey of thoughts, experiences, and senses.

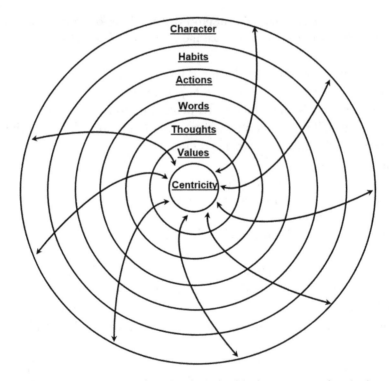

Fig. 4.1 The dynamic concept of Spiritual Leadership (source: own drawing)

I am starting from the "Talmud" or Lao Tzu (Lǎozǐ 老子), extending it to a level beyond, the level of values. Beyond this deeper level of values lies the true core of Spiritual Leadership: inner Centricity as the powerful source of everything that lies above it. That is the way to come to the following *dynamic* concept of Spiritual Leadership as depicted in Fig. 4.1 (and I will explain in the following why it is a dynamic concept).

The different levels or layers of our person, our personality, of our Self, are interconnected. Working on one level of it will also have an effect on other levels above and below the level you currently work on, so that a dynamic multilevel process of continuous improvement is possible.

If you are able to read German, then I can very much recommend you the book of Bernhard Moestl in "Denken wie ein Shaolin—die sieben Prinzipien emotionaler Selbstbestimmung" (Moestl 2016). In this book he explains interconnections on several levels, namely that how we think (i.e., our thoughts) is influencing and forming our decisions (i.e., our actions), our attitude (i.e., our habits), and our character.

This approach follows a similar understanding like the "Two Finger Smile" that Thomas Späth and Shi Yan Bao describe in their book "Shaolin—Das Geheimnis der inneren Stärke" "(Späth and Bao 2011, another German book which I can highly recommend to readers with German language knowledge):

A meditation teacher gave the monks in his Shaolin monastery the task to start each day with a smile, in order to bring joy and happiness into every day of their life. Some days this worked well; however, some other days it turned out to be difficult, as the monks were tired, or in a bad mood. Therefore, their teacher advised them to stand in front of a mirror, look at their own face, put their index fingers at their mouth angles, and push them up into a simile. The effect:

By actively making their mouth smile and seeing their own smile, their body, mind, and spirit adopted this smile and created a state of increasing happiness. This may sound strange, however: it really works!

There is even a therapy called "smile therapy." Those of you who had—just like myself—enjoyed watching the US TV series Ally McBeal may remember it *(Kelley, 1997–2002)*, as in that TV series, the senior partner lawyer John Cage tries this therapy on himself. Like the Shaolin monk practice, this therapy uses a practice of actively smiling physically, with the effect that—by a body–mind correlation—the actively smiling person also mentally and emotionally gets happier.

Conclusion for Your Leadership

The concept of Spiritual Leadership is focusing on what you can *learn about your Self* and how you can *work on your Self, with full consciousness and Awareness*. In other words, expressing it with the (alleged) wisdom of or Lao Tzu or Talmud:

Watch your Character.
Watch your Habits.
Watch your Actions.
Watch your Words.
Watch your Thoughts.
Watch your Values.
Finally, at the core of it:
Watch your inner Centricity.

References

Kelley DE (director) (1997–2002) Ally McBeal. TV-Series
Moestl B (2016) Denken wie ein Shaolin – Die sieben Prinzipien emotionaler Selbstbestimmung. Knaur, München
Späth T, Bao SY (2011) Shaolin – Das Geheimnis der inneren Stärke. Gräfe und Unzer, München
Wikipedia (2018) Concept. Wikipedia the free encyclopedia. https://en.wikipedia.org/wiki/Concept. Accessed May 22, 2018

5

Where to Start?

The good news: you can start on any level of the Spiritual Leadership concept to work on yourself, on your Self. No matter which level you work on, there will always be a learning effect for yourself, and finally for your Self. Therefore, wherever you start, it will always be an enrichment for yourself, and it can be a motivation for a life-long journey of learning.

The bad news: the deeper you go, the more effective it will be, but the harder it becomes to work on it.

There is an old Chinese proverb, still well known in China today, because Mao Zedong apparently often used to cite it. This proverb goes (see also Fig 5.1):

Huó dào lăo.
  Xué dào lăo.

which means

Live until old,
  Learn until old.

This essentially expresses the aforementioned life-long journey of learning, as there is always more and new things to discover and to learn in our life. Especially in our era of worldwide connectivity and globalization, we have access to endless resources of knowledge of all humankind, worldwide, and of all cultures. An enormous source of knowledge and wisdom, a source that our ancestors would never have dared to dream of. However, it takes a long time,

T. H. Ulrich, *Spiritual Leadership*, https://doi.org/10.1007/978-3-030-45432-6_5

Fig. 5.1 Calligraphy Huó dào lǎo, xué dào lǎo 活到老, 学到老 (Source: own photo, calligraphy ordered and purchased myself in China)

maybe our whole life, to identify, learn, and to focus onto what is truly important for us, to "digest" it and let it have an effect in and an impact onto our life.

So do not be frustrated when—after reading this book—you will not experience an immediate effect. Take your time. This is also part of the learning. Good things need time to develop. Allow yourself this time and freedom.

I am convinced—from my own experience—that a lot of what you may wish to learn, in fact is already there, in your own life, right in front of you, or even inside yourself. You may just have to consciously recognize it, distill it from the things that cover it, that hide it. To distill it from the things that keep your mind busy all the time. It is about developing Consciousness, Awareness, and Mindfulness. In order to develop your own motto of a life-long journey of learning, in a sense:

> Learn from your Life,
>   to Learn for your Life.

Why is this understanding, this mindset of continuous, life-long learning so essential for a Leader? My father often reminded me that you could even learn from the most ignorant persons (literally he used to say, "You can even learn from the most stupid"). This is an expression of modesty, a modesty of the wise, who understands and recognizes the limitations and inadequacies of every human being, and appreciates the very personal and individual knowledge that every person, every human being possesses. We can already find this understanding, this cognition in the book Tao Te King (Dàodéjīng 道德经) of Lao Tzu (Lǎozǐ 老子) which dates back to the sixth century B.C., and which reads (in one possible translation):

> To be wise, you do not have to know many things.
>   One, who knows many things, is not yet wise.

Modern Leadership theories now pick up this understanding again, developing the concept of Knower–Learner Mindset, in a sense:

- The (self)understanding of a (continuously learning) Learner
- In contrast to the understanding of the (already knowing) Knower

as laid out by Allan Milham and Guy Parsons in their book "Out of the Question: How Curious Leaders Win" (Milham and Parsons 2014) and on their Website www.thecuriousleader.com.

Continuous, life-long learning, openness for learning in and from each situation of life, and the personal exchange with every person, every human being—be it in business life in our function as a Leader, or be it in private life—will always be an enrichment for us as a person, and it is the essential basis of mutual understanding. Because understanding requires to really "learn about each other" in order to "get to know each other."

To express it very clearly: It is not about talking down knowledge. Because knowledge (in the sense of know-how and expertise) is more than ever the basis of entrepreneurial success. However, "seeming knowledge" or "assumed knowledge" is a danger, because if we think we know without really knowing, then we are (often unconsciously) "shutting ourselves off" behind assumptions with respect to what is actually happening around us. Especially in a situation that would require true and open communication, relying on our knowledge rather than being open for learning is risky, as then we tend to miss—or even to be deaf for—what our counterpart really says and what truly drives him.

The "Learner," on the other hand, is someone who listens impartially, who asks instead of presuming or knowing, in order to learn and to get to know. He is someone who actively asks back, in order to learn, to truly get to know what his counterpart really means. As to myself, I took the habit in interviews with candidates who apply for a job to deliberately ask in detail what my counterpart meant by certain terms or statements.

Example: The candidate may say, "For me, team spirit and respect are very important". Then I would ask back "what exactly do you mean by 'team spirit' and how can you describe your personal understanding of 'respect' for me in more detail?" Quite often, a much clearer picture emerged about the candidate from such conversation that goes deeper beyond the superficial level, and strengths emerged that the candidate—perhaps out of nervousness—did not express so clearly. On the other hand, also weaknesses emerged that were essential for my decision in favor of or against the hiring candidate.

Today we also talk a lot about "diversity" in companies, in a sense of appreciating diversity of people, of human beings in every sense. It is exactly this diversity of human beings that—in my understanding—requires our openness and curiosity for, and an active approach toward, the wide variety of human characters and cultures. We must first be willing to get to know who our counterpart is and what drives him, what is important for him, what characterizes him, what affects him, and where his pain points are. This requires an openness for learning, so that *"Learning"* can lead to *"true Knowing."* In the next chapter, we will learn more about the importance of *"true knowing"* of the characteristics of an individual, of a *"true Knowing"* that arises from impartial and unbiased "Learning."

One may object that "Knowing" is not truly necessary, because quite often we can very well rely on our "gut feeling." Yes, from my own experience I can confirm that the own "gut feeling" can be a very good guidance, for a Leader in a company as well as in our everyday private life. Especially when there is a bad "gut feeling" that does not go away, when there is a permanent uncomfortable feeling in a certain situation or with respect to a certain decision. This gut feeling is not without a reason or without a deeper source. Rather, it arises from the sum of our own experience, knowledge, emotions that we have gathered—consciously or unconsciously—throughout our life. It is based on what we have learned during our whole life, and what we have learned from our life. It means that "gut feeling" can actually be a good guidance, because it is based on extensive learning and the total of our knowledge, on everything that defines us, and on what is essential for ourselves.

Conclusion for Your Leadership

You can start on any level of the Spiritual Leadership concept to work on yourself, on your Self. No matter which level you work on, there will always be a learning effect for yourself, and finally for your Self.

However, the deeper you go, the more effective it will be, but the harder it becomes to work on it.

It will nevertheless be a constant enrichment for yourself, for your Self, and it can be a motivation for a life-long journey of continuous Learning.

Therefore:

Keep on learning.
    Learn from your Life,
    To Learn for your Life.

References

Lao Tzu (Lǎozǐ 老子), Tao Te King (Dàodéjīng 道德经), 6th Century B.C., e.g. in Wing RL (1999) Der Weg und die Kraft, Tao-te-king, Bechtermünz, Augsburg

Milham A, Parsons G (2014) Out of question: how curious leaders win. Advantage Media Group, Charleston

Website. www.thecuriousleader.com. Accessed May 22, 2018

6

Via Character to Centricity

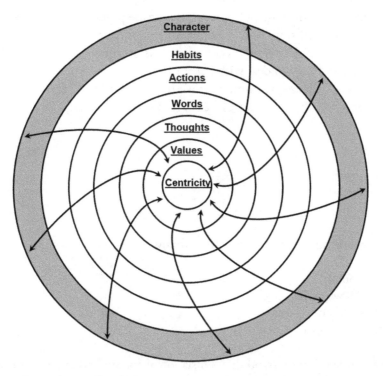

Character (source: own drawing)

Let us start on the outer level, from the Character. We can find a definition of the expression "Character", for example, in the Wikipedia encyclopedia:

Character is an evaluation of an individual's stable moral qualities. The concept of character can imply a variety of attributes including the existence or lack of virtues such as empathy, courage, fortitude, honesty, and loyalty, or of good behaviors or habits. Moral character primarily refers to the assemblage of qualities that distinguish one individual from another. (Wikipedia 2018a)

Therefore, your Character is something very stable, long-lasting, and due to this, your Character is "characterizing" you as a person, or better: as a personality. It is kind of an "overall summary" of your personality, the outer and tangible appearance of your personality. The Character of a person is quite easy to identify for others who have a good sense for people. For yourself it is quite easy to get an understanding of how your Character is perceived by others—you may simply ask others to give you a feedback on your character, in order to crosscheck with your self-perception of your character. Such feedback and alignment with your self-perception can help you to consciously focus and center yourself onto your Character as a source of power (Later on, we will have a look at what "real" feedback means, in the sense of qualified feedback means and how to deal with it.).

There is a Chinese wisdom, a proverb from Sun Tsu "The Art of War" (Sūnzi Bīngfǎ 孙子兵法; Sun Tsu 2007), that reads (see Fig. 6.1):

Zhī jǐ
    zhī bǐ
    bǎi zhàn
    bǎi sheng
    (Tsu, 500 B.C)

This proverb is usually translated as follows:

Know yourself
    and know your enemy,
    then a hundred battles
    will turn into a hundred victories.

As to myself, I understand this translation as too limited and too much limited to the military background, from which Sūnzi Bīngfǎ was obviously derived. I prefer the following translation in a wider sense that—to my understanding—better reflects the deeper meaning of the proverb in the Chinese sense:

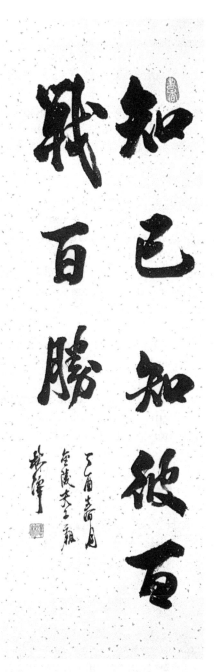

Fig. 6.1   Calligraphy Zhī jǐ zhī bǐ bǎi zhàn bǎi shèng 知己知彼百戰百勝, (Source: own photo, calligraphy ordered and purchased myself in China)

Know yourself
  and know your counterpart,
  then a hundred conflicts
  will turn into a hundred successes.

This has been for already a long time a guideline in my life, which has developed—from a professional strategic guideline in business life—into a general guideline for my whole life, both for my professional as well as for my private life. Because this wisdom is generally applicable, whether it is about the cooperation between yourself as a leader and your team member, your boss, or your colleague as a professional counterpart, or about the relationship in your family, between yourself and your family members as your private counterparts. In any personal situation, *true knowledge* of the Character— your own Character and the Character of your counterpart—is essential for avoiding or eliminating conflicts and for mutual success.

The same also applies to the entrepreneurial business world of—and between—companies:

- Only if you know the Character of your own company, its strategy, its organization, its strengths and weaknesses, its products and its technologies,
- and if you know the Character of your competitors, i.e. their strategies, their organization, their strengths and their weaknesses, their products and their technologies (of course only on the basis of legally acquired information!),
- only then will you be able to persist in the competition in today's global markets,
- and turn (possible) conflicts into successes.

My personal experience and understanding: Many seemingly complex business strategies and business planning can be reduced to this very simple concept:

Know yourself
  and know your counterpart.

What remains are the operational questions: which methods, processes, core competences, tools, and support are required to successfully cover these two aspects.

In the following, I would like to focus on applying and using this wisdom for the understanding of our individual Character and to look at it in a broader context. For this proverb is embedded into a wider context in Sun Tsu "The Art of War" (Sūnzi Bīngfǎ), which reads:

One who knows himself
   but not his counterpart,
   for every success gained
   he will also suffer a defeat.
One who knows neither himself
   nor his counterpart,
   will succumb in every conflict

In the previous chapter, I already pointed out how important it is to have a mindset of continuous learning, to get to know via learning, not to act as a Knower, but as a Learner. Such wisdom can already be found in philosophical literature even before Sun Tsu "The Art of War", namely in Tao Te King (Dàodéjīng 道德经), originating from Lao Tzu (Lǎozǐ 老子) in the sixth century B.C.:

Knowing others is intelligence,
   knowing yourself is true wisdom.
   Mastering others is strength,
   mastering yourself is true power.

To know what you stand for, to know your own Character, to know what is important for yourself and how your own Self "ticks" (or what makes you "tick" in a certain manner), and also to know the Character of the persons around you, all of this is an essential basis for a Leader. It is essential in order to achieve success and positive performance for yourself and for others, for your team, your organization, or your company. We will come back to this in a later chapter, when we will talk about feedback as a means to determine your own position.

But how can you consciously draw strength from your understanding of your own Character? Let us first understand where the term "Character" comes from:

The word goes back to ancient Greek χαρακτήρ charaktér and originally means "embossed stamp" or "coinage" [as an imprint or mark on a coin], and in a figurative sense also "idiosyncrasy.". (translated from Wikipedia 2018b)

This meaning of the word "character" in the sense of a visible and permanent "mark" leads us to a possibility of how to literally visualize your Character for yourself, to focus on it, and develop a Centricity of mind around it:

Of course you can chose different ways in order to determine and to "characterize" a Character—be it your own Character or the Character of your counterpart. For example, Walter Rotter describes a method in his book "Der Charakterleser—Wer Du bist und wie Du mehr aus Dir machst" (Rotter

2016) of how to "decrypt" a specific, individual Character—especially your own Character—by deriving it from 288 basic types of Characters. He also explains how to impact and leverage your further development by making use of this understanding of your own Character. Be it to develop more charisma as a Leader, be it for further development of your own personality.

In the following, I would like to propose you a different way that does not require such complex approach using a big number of Character stereotypes:

Find yourself a Totem!

Why a Totem? What does that mean? Let us look at a definition of Totem:

"A totem is a symbol or a spirit that represents and watches over a group of people." (Wikipedia 2018c)

In many cultures, people are choosing or being given a kind of Totem or Symbol: visible or visualized Totems or Symbols, like American Indian Totems in the form of animal symbols that are intended to represent a person or his Character, or intended to inspire him. However, also non-visible Totems or symbols like nicknames or so-called "war names" of soldiers or gang fighters. You may remember the movie "Top Gun" where Tom Cruise plays the character Pete Mitchell who has the war name "Maverick," as he in fact is a maverick Character for a long time in this movie. His competitor in the Top Gun squadron is Tom Kazanski, war name "Iceman." I assume you can already guess his Character in case you do not know the movie (any more). Moreover, we can find much more of these characteristic war names in the movie. And the most exciting thing is to see how these people, these Characters develop during the movie and ultimately "win" by leaving their old Character, leaving their comfort zone, and thereby growing beyond it, beyond themselves.

Totems can be very powerful. Most prominent is probably the already mentioned use of Totems in American Indian culture, and we probably all know it from Wild West movies where American Indian tribes play a role. However, I would like to have a look at a different example: In Harry Potter and the Prisoner of Azkaban, there is one magic spell that is one of the most powerful: the Patronus charm (Rowling 2014). This Patronus charm is a defensive spell, and in fact, it evokes a "Totem" animal. However, in order to be able to evoke this Patronus charm, the wizard or witch must find something deep inside himself or herself muster the happiest memory they can think of. Therefore, the success of this charm is linked to a very deep truth inside the person. Accordingly, the Totem animal of the Patronus charm is a symbol for the Character and qualities of the respective person: The Patronus of Harry Potter is a stag, that of Albus Dumbledore is a phoenix, and the Patronus of Hermione Granger is an otter. These animals represent essential traits of the corresponding person and its personality: independence, charisma, and strength (Potter)—wisdom, hope, and magical energy of life (almost) up to immortality (Dumbledore)—creativity, individualism, and freethinking (Granger).

Sometimes it is up to yourself to choose or to find a Totem or symbol for yourself, by chance or with full consciousness. Sometimes others find such Totem or symbol for you, such as a nickname with a real and deeper meaning. If, for example, you have business contacts with Asia, especially to China, then it can happen that your Chinese counterparts will give you a Chinese name. If it is well and carefully chosen, then your Chinese counterparts will assign you a name where the given name has a very personal meaning. In my case, a Chinese colleague—with whom I had established a Chinese-German language tandem in order to jointly improve our language skills of the respective other language—gave me a very precious farewell gift when he left for a different job in our company group:

He chose for me the following Chinese name as transliteration of my last name Ulrich into Chinese: Wú Lǐxián—吴礼贤, which has a meaning in the sense of: "the courteous able and virtuous person" or in short: "the courteous savant." You can imagine that I was very moved and proud to receive this meaningful name as a gift from my colleague. I got myself a necklace with this name on it, so that this necklace can remind me of the qualities that others see in me. Also in a later chapter of this book, you will encounter this name again.

Therefore, under the concept of Spiritual Leadership, a Totem is a symbol that represents yourself, or better: your Self, your Character, your qualities. Once you found a Totem for yourself, you can focus on it, look at it like looking into a mirror, and answer for yourself to the following questions:

How am I really?
What is my Character?
What are the strengths, what are the weaknesses of this Character?

It can help you to draw power and energy from it for yourself, whenever you may feel unsure of your Self.

Maybe you already have such a Totem or symbol, without being consciously aware of what it really means to you: do you have objects that you carry with you all the time like bracelets, necklaces or chain hangers, special key chains, or tattoos? If so, are you consciously aware of what they mean for you? Ask yourself what they symbolize for you, what do they stand for?

For myself, I was wearing a Buddhist Mala, a Buddhist prayer beads, as a bracelet for quite a long time. First, I did so without being fully aware of what it really means for me. Even when people asked me about it, I could not really answer it. I just felt it was important for me to wear it. Now I am wearing it with full consciousness, as it reminds me of what Buddhist way of life stands for—although I would not call myself a religious Buddhist. For myself, it is more a symbol of Awareness and Mindfulness, a symbol for the way to treat other human beings. Wearing it calls this understanding back to my conscience every day. Even if in reality I repeatedly fail to practice what the Mala should remind me of, as like everybody, I am just a fallible human being. Nevertheless, there is also potential and power in failure, and later on we will look deeper into the issue of how to deal with failure.

Exercise on Centricity

Let your subconscious choose a Totem or Symbol for yourself (or better: for your Self): wander through some department stores, flea markets, jewelry markets, etc. and just listen to your gut feeling: what attracts your interest, like some kind of magnetic force attracting a metal object?

In order to actually and truly feel such attraction, I recommend that you test out real objects in real shops or markets and not in online shops. So that you can see, feel, perceive, and literally "grasp" the objects as they really are. This is a much more "real" and effective way than relying on photoshop beautified online representations, which easily turn the attraction into disappointment when the item is actually delivered to your home by mail.

If such attraction happens, ask yourself:

What does that object stand for?

Why does it feel important for me?

Which of my qualities, what part of my Character, of my Self does it represent?

When you find answers to these questions, then you have done a first step toward Centricity.

You may find this insight still somewhat superficial. You are right. As we have just touched the outermost level on our way, our journey towards the core of inner Centricity, I promise you: The insights and impacts will become deeper with each level.

Conclusion for Your Leadership

Your Character is something very stable, long-lasting, it is "characterizing" you—and every other human being—as a person, or better: as a personality. It is kind of an "overall summary" of your personality. The Character of a person is quite easy to identify for others who have a good sense for people. To consciously focus yourself onto your Character as a source of power can help you to be centered and to draw strength for yourself from this understanding. To understand and to know your own Character and the Character of your counterparts is the basis for success as a Leader, in line with the thousands of years old wisdom of Sun Tsu:

> Know yourself
>   and know your counterpart,
>   then a hundred conflicts
>   will turn into a hundred successes.

This wisdom picks up the understanding of continuous learning of the previous chapter, so that "Learning" can become "Knowing." It shows the importance of "truly Knowing" the qualities of an individual, which results from impartial and unbiased "Learning."

This wisdom also applies to the Character of companies, to their strategy, and their organization. It can be a basis for success in the worldwide competition with other companies in today's global markets.

References

Rotter W (2016) Der Charakterleser – Wer Du bist und wie Du mehr aus Dir machst. Goldmann, München

Rowling JK (2014) Harry Potter and the Prisoner of Azkaban. Bloomsbury Children's Books, London

Sun Tsu " The Art of War" (Sūnzi Bīngfǎ 孙子兵法), about 500 B.C., e.g.in: Luo Zhiye (translator), (2007), Sun Tzu's The Art of War, Chinese Classical Treasury (Chinese-Englisch Edition), Zhongguo Chuban Jituan, Beijing, ISBN 978-7-5001-1812-1

Wikipedia (2018a) Moral character. Wikipedia The Free Encyclopedia. https://en.wikipedia.org/wiki/Moral_character. Accessed May 22, 2018

Wikipedia (2018b) Charakter. Wikipedia Die freie Enzyklopädie. https://de.wikipedia.org/wiki/Charakter. Accessed May 22, 2018

Wikipedia (2018c) Totem. Wikipedia The Free Encyclopedia. https://en.wikipedia.org/wiki/Totem. Accessed May 22, 2018

7

Via Habits to Centricity

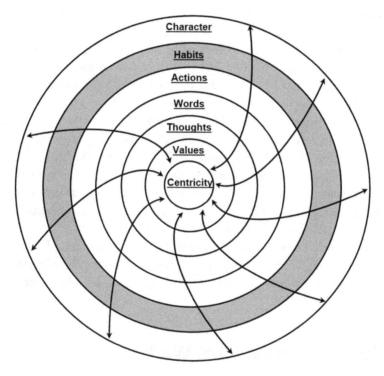

Habits (source: own drawing)

Let us start again by first clarifying the meaning of the word. In encyclopedias like Wikipedia, you can find a definition of Habit as follows:

> A habit (also usus, lat. Uti "use") is a reaction mode developed under similar conditions, which has been stereotyped by repetition and, under similar situation conditions, is automatically carried out according to the same reaction scheme if it is not consciously avoided or suppressed. (translated from: Wikipedia 2018)

So when talking about Habits, it is not about a singular action or a one-time behavior. It is about a general way of acting. It is about how we "use to do things." In other words: it is about role behavior. Although Habits tend to occur unconsciously, we can nevertheless consciously reflect on our Habits, i.e., reflect on roles and other general ways of acting that we are used to.

As already pointed out, Stefan Wachtel deals in his book "Sei nicht authentisch—warum klug manchmal besser ist als echt" with a conscious way of reflecting on the own roles of a person, and working on appropriate or expected role behavior (Wachtel 2014). Wachtel recommends that you do a conscious analysis of the expectations of others with regard to your own role, and advises to consciously adapt your own appearance and behavior to the expectations of others for this role in order to improve your personal impact in the respective role. So it is about deliberately reflecting on a role and focusing on what that role is. In his newer book "Executive Modus—12 Taktiken für mehr Führungswirkung" (Wachtel 2017), Wachtel focuses even more specifically on how managers can work on a professional appearance—especially with regard to their own communication—in order to be truly perceived as an executive instead of, e.g., being perceived as an expert only.

In this section, I would like to address some types of roles, Habits, or general ways of acting which—already by consciously putting them into the focus of your self-perception—can help to be more focused and centric in our behavior.

Habits in Organization of Work

In the organization of our work, especially in the operative organization of processes and tasks, our Habits can tend to mislead us in a way that takes away our efficiency and our Focus. So how to overcome this inherent danger that lies in our own Habits? The only way is to actively focus on and recognize our Habits, and change our Habits if they mislead us. For this, we can find some "first aid" in some popular publications.

For example, in the book "The One Minute Manager Meets The Monkey," (Blanchard 2000) the authors Kenneth Blanchard and William Oncken point out how important it is to consciously organize an appropriate assignment of tasks in a team and to establish for yourself a habit of "Monkey Management." Such "Monkey Management" is about clearly understanding, defining, and assigning tasks ("monkeys") to the right person in a team, especially when you are in the role of a manager or Leader being responsible for such assignments. Otherwise, you may easily find yourself trapped in a habit of a "white knight syndrome" who in the end has put most of the "monkey" burden onto his own shoulders. Failure—in the negative, destructive sense of the expression— is nearly inevitable for a Leader if doing so (We will get to know later that there can also be failure in the constructive sense).

What the authors Blanchard and Oncken explain in their book means no less than how important it is for yourself to get used to developing a Habit of questioning, recognizing, and clearly defining responsibilities in the team and to get people "in charge." Ultimately, everyone in the team, including the team members, benefit from it, because by clearly defining and assigning responsibilities and getting team members in charge, the team members become accustomed to—and develop a Habit of—taking over responsibility for their tasks (for their monkeys).

Therefore, it is very important to develop and strengthen Focus in our Habits, in organization of work and tasks. Be focused and centric in the tasks that are your own, and give tasks that belong to others in your team, to those in your team who they really belong to, so that they themselves become focused on their own tasks. This may of course lead to some irritations in the beginning. However, in the long run you will experience a rise in motivation in your team and a rise in energy, power, and Centricity in yourself.

With this, we come to an often-discussed question: What is it that really motivates people? I have myself experienced the following in the Leadership mentoring and assessment centers that I have been in as a mentor or assessment observer: when you talk to Leaders, especially to young people in a Leadership role, and ask them "what are your tasks as a Leader," one frequent answer is "to motivate my team." However, what does that mean? Is it really necessary to *actively motivate* people? It appears like forcing people to drink from a source of energy and inspiration. Since quite some time, I have doubted that this is true. And then, from a video of Dan Pink featuring RSA Animate "Drive: the surprising truth about what motivates us" (Dan Pink, RSA Animate 2010) on a study conducted by the MIT (Massachusetts Institute of Technology), I understood: Motivation comes automatically when we as a Leader:

- Become aware of what the people in our team are good at,
- Even further seek to strengthen their natural skills and encourage them to use them,
- And give our people freedom in what they really like to do and are good at,
- Because then they are completely centered in their true being and free to move around this "personal center of gravity".

According to Dan Pink, and according the findings he derived from the study conducted by MIT, three factors really motivate people, namely:

Autonomy, Mastery, and Purpose.

This is the essence of what really motivates our team members, our people, and us. Therefore, if—as a Leader—we create a Habit of conscious Focus on these success factors, for giving our people Autonomy, Mastery, and Purpose, then we will create an environment for our team, where motivation will unfold all by itself.

In their book "Ikigai—The Japanese Secret to a Long and Happy Life," the authors Héctor García and Francesc Miralles (García and Miralles 2017) explain a Japanese concept and understanding of the importance to have a core purpose in life, in Japanese Ikigai (生き甲斐) which means "a reason for being." Finding the own Ikigai is seen as a core aspect to lead a long and happy life. It is the reason for being, the passion, and vocation that the Ikigai gives to the one who was able to find it for himself, to perceive it and to focus on it, to put it at the Center of his own life and being.

Habits in Living Your Role as a Leader

As a Leader, we usually—consciously or unconsciously—live a certain Role depending on the specific situation. We cannot avoid it. We even live different Roles in different contexts: in business life, in private life, in the family, with our friends, in our sports team.

The more you are aware of your current role and current role behavior, and the more you live it with full consciousness, the more you will *BE* this Role.

The Role will become a natural and authentic part of your Self. The more authentic you are in your Role, the more people around you will be willing to accept you as a natural and authentic Leader.

As mentioned, Stefan Wachtel points out in his book "Sei nicht authentisch" (Wachtel 2014) how important it is to be aware of what people expect from you in your Role and advises to consciously fulfil these expectations, which means to adapt yourself—your Self—to this Role. Therefore, the approach of Stefan Wachtel is coming from a rather extrinsic motivation, i.e. fulfilling external expectations, which helps to develop a consciously created appearance of Authenticity. However, I see the risk that such consciously constructed appearance of Authenticity might be perceived as artificial. Many human beings have a quite good sense for "real" or "fake" behavior.

To my understanding, we must go to a deeper level of Leadership Roles and Leadership Habits, beyond an extrinsic motivation toward an intrinsic motivation, toward an understanding and focus of our Leadership Role and habits that come from deep inside. To do so, we first need to understand our true Role, understand what that Role means for ourselves, for our Self, how we fit into that Role. Only then, we can develop for ourselves a picture, an analogy of our Role, and then identify ourselves with the role we represent in our team environment.

It is important for you to understand, define, and find yourself in your appropriate Role, coming from your inner Self(understanding), and to turn that Role into your Habit. By truly finding your understanding of the roles and Habits that really "match yourself—your Self" and literally visualizing yourself into the center of that Role, you can develop a powerful impact on the people around you without "tumbling around."

There is an Asian wisdom (source unknown, sometimes said to be originating from Lao Tzu), which reads:

Nothing is closer to you than yourself.
But if you do not know yourself, then how would you know others?

In the following passages, I will describe for you some examples of Leadership Role pictures, in order to give you a better understanding what this concept of developing a picture of your own Leadership Role and visualizing yourself into the center of that role means.

To give you a comparison: In his book "Team Roles at Work" (Belbin 1993), R. Meredith Belbin differentiates between team Roles—in the sense of behavior within the team and among the team members—and technical Roles—i.e., the technical tasks. I do not want to make such a detailed distinction here, already for the mere fact that, in my experience, in business reality there is no real separation between team (member) behavior and professional tasks. Rather, technical tasks and behavior in the team are (at least partially) mutually dependent, i.e., depending on our technical task in the team. We adapt our behavior within a team, and depending on our behavior, we get—at least gradually—corresponding technical tasks. Alternatively, we are hired for certain technical tasks in a team based on our behavior during the job interview. Similar, in a negative outcome scenario, we do not get a certain job in a team because our behavior during the job interview was not as expected.

Leadership Roles Versus Roles in Football (Soccer)

One picture of a Leadership Role that very much helped me in my business life—both for myself and my own understanding of my Leadership Role, as well as in communicating and transmitting a tangible picture of my Leadership Role to others, to superiors, peers, and team members—is the analogy of football (in the United States: soccer, Fig. 7.1). Another analogy would be that of a captain on a ship.

I very much like the analogy of football, as many people know football and the Roles involved (at least in Europe). On the other hand, an analogy in a

Fig. 7.1 Roles in a team (source: www.pixabay.com, created by geralt, amended)

Fig. 7.2 Role as a referee (source: www.pixabay.com, created by Free-Photos, amended)

domain different to that of our ordinary professional life creates a certain distance to the Leadership Role in the job, which makes it easier to look at things more objectively and therefore easier to understand. In addition, valuable experiences and insights from one sphere of our life can also be helpful and enriching for other spheres of our life. As there is always one thing at the Center, at the core of each of these spheres: that is ourselves, our Self.

Typical and characteristic Roles in football are:

- The different players of the team (Team-Players)
- The captain of the team (leading Team-Player at the Center of the Team)
- The coach of the team (Team-Coach)
- A combination of coach and player in one person (Player-Coach)—often in small teams where a pure Team-Coach is not justifiable or available
- A decider to make sure that rules are obeyed and to control and lead the game by decision taking (Referee, Fig. 7.2)

Typically, Leaders of bigger teams and/or on higher organization levels will combine at least two Roles in their Leadership: that of a Team-Coach and that of a decider (Referee), as:

1. On the one hand, such Leaders have typical tasks of a Team-Coach, namely tasks of team organization and team management, in particular:

   - Defining the positions/Roles in the team as well as the characteristics of and required competences for those positions/Roles in the team (in football for example: attackers, mid-field players, defenders, and a goal keeper, with even more sub-Role varieties within these main Roles)

- Finding and hiring the right persons for those positions/Roles that best match the characteristics and competences of the respective position/ Role (highly sophisticated attackers, versatile mid-field players, down-to-earth tough defenders that support the others from the background and a goal keeper that does everything to "keep your backyard clean") and

- Keeping in mind that, when thinking about moving or even promoting persons to other positions/Roles, not every person is a good fit for every position/Role, so that you have to carefully select which players to move and when and how to move or promote players, and which player is not a candidate to be moved or promoted to a different position/Role, as his characteristics and competences simply do not match the required characteristics and competences of the respective position/Role as well as

2. In addition, such Leader has the typical tasks of a Referee, in particular:

- Decision-making, even in unclear situations, i.e., in situations where you do not have all the information available that you might wish to have to take the decision and

- Understanding that it is your role to lead the game by means of deciding, i.e., understanding that decisions are part of the game, including the risk of taking objectively "wrong" decisions, in a sense that later on, some so-called "outside experts" may prove to you with sophisticated techniques and technology that one or the other decision was not "right"

After developing for myself this picture of a Leadership Role in the analogy to football, I had done some research in literature and actually found a book that deals with key aspects of this topic, namely Reinhard K. Sprenger in his book "Gut aufgestellt—Fußballstrategien für Manager" (Sprenger 2008). He explains and clearly differentiates the Roles of a coach and a player or a team, respectively, using many examples from the history and practice of football, and points out—among other things—that a good player (expert in a certain position) and a good coach or trainer (Leader) are two different talents that are just not interchangeable. With this understanding, he is picking up a very important topic that we know well from our own Leadership and business experience:

In business world, however, we very often see that someone is promoted to a Leadership position, because he has proven himself a good expert (player) in his previous position. On the other hand, quite often experts (players) expect a promotion to a Leadership position after a certain time, just—and often for the only reason—because they did a good job in their position (which very often is true). Quite often, such promoted experts (players) fail in a Leadership position when such Role is not suitable for them. Especially because—once in the Leadership position—the promoted expert players tend to fall back into their previous, old patterns of expert activity and jump onto and dive into expert topics again whenever there is a chance to do so, instead of developing a Habit and a competence of Leadership, which is unsatisfactory, tragic, and frustrating in two ways, namely for themselves in their new Role as a Leader, and for the team that they should actually lead.

However, there is one aspect of a Leadership Role in the analogy to football Sprenger does not pick up, namely the aforementioned second Role, the Role of the Referee as driver of the game, by means of—quite often criticized—decisions and risk taking. However, this is also of great importance for an effective Leader in his Leadership Role.

Some years ago, I had the chance to follow an impressive speech of world class football referee Markus Merk on the topic of decision-making, and I can highly recommend the book of Urs Meier (another a world class referee) "Du bist die Entscheidung" (Meier 2010). Both have in common a very clear understanding of how important it is to learn to take quick and clear decisions, and to learn to accept and deal with the risks involved in decision-making. Both point out that it is often more important to be decisive, to take a decision (and to dare to take it), as well as taking the risk that the decision may later turn out to be "wrong," rather than seeking too long to find a solution that is absolutely "right," and while seeking delaying things for too long. It is also important to understand that decisions are a conscious personal act, required for a selection between more or less *equal alternatives* (like between two types of cake), not a confirmation of an analysis that already shows one solution to be clearly more advantageous than another (like between piece of cake and a piece of mud). Nevertheless, the latter is what quite often happens when "requests for decisions" are brought in front of decision committees in companies. Consequently, there is often no clear "right" or "wrong" in a real decision process. We will deal with the topic of risks and risk management in more detail later in this book.

Conclusion for Your Leadership

From an analogy, from a picture of typical Roles in a different environment (here in football), it is possible to:

- Develop a very clear and objective picture of a Leadership Role from a certain distance
- Get an understanding and helpful insights for team setup, team positions, and the associated required competences
- Develop an awareness for the importance of position-related selection of the best fitting players based on their true competences, and
- Understand the importance of decision taking and accepting the associated risks as a natural part of the game
- That is, to develop a deeper and more centered understanding and awareness for the aspects that are essential for success in a Leadership Role

Leadership Roles Versus Roles in a Family

Let us have a look at a further example of Role analogy. Another picture that has proven to be very helpful in my business life is the analogy of a family and the respective Roles in a family (Fig. 7.3). It helped to define and to focus on my own responsibilities and duties, as well as on my relationships to and

Fig. 7.3   Roles in a family (source: www.pixabay.com, created by Free-Photos, amended)

respective responsibilities and duties of superiors, peers, and team members. It even helped to define and to focus on relationships between legal entities of our company group.

The reason is that each of us has his or her own personal experience in a family, at least in the Role as a child, many also in the Role as parents (father or mother) with own children. Also in this picture, the analogy to a private life sphere creates an objectivizing distance to the business sphere and Leadership Role, and our experience and insights as children—and possibly also as parents—and ultimately our habits resulting from them, can be transferred to and applied in our Leadership Role.

Myself being for quite a many years in both Roles, as a father and as a Leader of a team, it was one of my most striking experiences to perceive and understand the parallels between my father Role and my Role as a Leader. On the other hand, I myself am—of course—also a son for my own parents, i.e., in a "subordinate" family Role; likewise, I always had other Leaders above me, to whom I was reporting to as a member of their respective team. On the same hierarchy level like myself, there were always peers of similar experience level, just as I have a brother who is of the same generation and of similar age in my own family. So in each of these spheres—in business life as well as in private life—I myself was and still am confronted with multiple Roles and representing multiple Roles myself:

- Father–Leader
- Brother–peer
- Son–direct report/team member

Therefore, it is about focusing, about being focused on what is our Role with respect to whom, and about consciously visualizing for ourselves the typical characteristics of this Role. This gives a much better and clearer basis to cross-check the understanding of the own Role with the expectations of other persons above, below, and around us.

As a Leader/father, being responsible for still growing or already mature team members/adult children, it is a core task and challenge to establish and constantly reinforce mutual trust, followed and accompanied by working constantly on the balance between the Habit of:

1. Helping the own team members/children to grow further, by more or less helping, supporting and guiding them on their way
   and

2. Giving the own team members/children reasonable and appropriate freedom, to allow and to enable them so that they can take over their own responsibility in their domains, can develop their own skills, and can gather their own experience

There is a lot to learn from one Role—e.g., as a father—which you can apply in your other Role—e.g., as a Leader—and vice versa, if you do it consciously, if you focus on it, and if it comes out of yourself, your Self. As many fathers/mothers probably know from their own experience, every child is different from the other: one is more independent, self-confident, and more "grown up" already after a short time, another remains adolescent for longer time, is more dependent on others, and not sure of himself—or of his Self. It is about understanding that each child needs an individual understanding, individual treatment, and individually adapted level of guidance or freedom. Each child needs individual focus and attention, needs our awareness. The same is true for the members of our team.

In both Roles, as father and as a Leader, there is the risk of overdoing either the one or the other: giving too much freedom and being too careless, or not giving enough freedom and over-caring. For the last way of overdoing, there is now even a specific expression: "helicopter parents," i.e., parents who are overprotecting their children, watching them all the time, taking every burden off their shoulders, and putting the burden on their own shoulders (Do you remember the "Monkey Management" described previously?). The effect of it is that the parent later complains about how immature their children are and that the children may either not develop an own sense of responsibility or may try everything to escape from the surveillance and lack of freedom at home. Sometimes, conscious Not Doing, not acting is more helpful and more targeted than (over)doing. We will come back to the point of Not Doing later in this book.

Also for the understanding of reasonable intragroup, intercompany relationship of our organizations within Bosch Group, the analogy of a family was very helpful. Myself as a responsible Leader of a Corporate team of a Bosch subgroup (i.e., a "daughter company group"), I had to find, define, and focus on my Role and relationship with the overall global Bosch Group Corporate Leader who represents the interest of the Bosch Group mother company. So what does a mother company expect of a daughter company and vice versa? It is again about establishing and constantly reinforcing mutual trust, and about finding an appropriate balance between:

(a) Living the own freedom as an adult daughter, based on the trust of the mother in her daughter that the daughter will to abuse this freedom

(b) Being aware and respecting the core interests of the mother where she is the appropriate (legal)person to set the global directions, rules, and standards for the whole family

(c) Involving the mother when certain things may become important, difficult, or risky for the whole family

Being consciously aware of such a picture and analogy, and consciously and mindfully focusing on the Roles and habits within such picture, can allow us a much bigger impact in our Leadership Role, without "tumbling around," as we are fully aligned with our Center and can remain much more stable while the masses are moving around us.

Leadership Roles: Dictator Versus Team Diversity

If you are a movie fan rather than a football fan or family person, you may find the following analogies more inspiring. I would like to address two Leadership characters, both popular from Science Fiction movies/TV series (at least for my generation), and both quite different from each other.

The Dictator—Darth Vader

A very striking example of a Dictator leader is Darth Vader (Fig. 7.4) (Lucas 1977). Typical about the Dictator is that he has all the power in his hands. A powerful—but lonely—Leader. Darth Vader's power is so powerful that he can even kill people with a thought—preferably subordinates who did not do their job well. People follow him because they are afraid of his power (the "Dark Side of the Force"), and the last thing his subordinates would do is acting beyond the orders they have received, as doing so could cause maximum harm to them: it could cost them their lives. I assume you know how the story ends: Darth Vader—despite his power, despite an army of well-trained men, and powerful weapons at his disposal—loses the decisive battle against some desperate but highly motivated rebels, and finally, the Center of his power—the Death Star—gets destroyed.

You may ask yourself: what is the weak point about such an obviously powerful Leader? Let us have a look at how literature deals with issues of power and Leadership.

Fig. 7.4 Darth Vader (source: www.pixabay.com, created by toxi85, amended)

Bernhard Moestl's book "Die 13 Siegel der Macht—Von der Kunst der guten Führung" (Moestl 2011) deals with the questions of how power arises, how it can be achieved, and how it can be retained. He derives his theses from historical examples and historical facts, combined with wisdom of East Asian philosophy. He takes a similar approach in his other book "Denken wie ein Shaolin—Die sieben Prinzipien emotionaler Selbstbestimmung" (Moestl 2016) which I can as well recommend to those able to read German, a book based on Chinese philosophy the fighting monks of the Shaolin monastery. Moestl thereby gives a Leader a "tool kit" to actively work on his power and understand his own power more deeply, penetrate its essence, and adapt its use appropriately. Moestl advises his readers in particular to focus and to live power consciously, to develop an awareness for it. Earlier in this book, we have already come across the principles of focus and awareness as one of the essential foundations of Leadership, and will hear more about them hereinafter.

However, as the example of the Dictator Leader Darth Vader shows us, power alone is obviously not enough to actually turn a Leader into a (permanently) effective and successful Leader. So let us have a further look at the insights in Leadership literature.

In his book "Team Roles at Work," Belbin describes the contrasting Leadership roles of a "single (solo) Leader" as opposed to a "team Leader" (Belbin 1993). Belbin sees it—among other things—as characteristic for a "solo Leader" that such a type of Leader strives for uniformity among his subordinates. Anyone who knows Star Wars is well aware that the army of Darth Vader is characterized by a high level of uniformity. Such uniformity exists among his direct (still human) subordinates, and even more so in the forces of clone warriors: an army of command receivers and command executers, practically without own will and without own Character or individuality, i.e., forces that are at the service of the Leader without any trait of opposition. It is exactly this extreme gap between the lonely, (all) powerful Leader and his uniform, powerless and will-less subordinates that—despite superiority in all "hard facts" (Key Performance Indicators KPIs)—actually causes a severe weakness of the dictator Leadership Role.

Therefore, an alternative Leadership Role is presented in the following section, namely that of the team Leader who derives his Leadership strength from team diversity.

Team Diversity—James T. Kirk

An extreme opposite to the Dictator Leadership of Darth Vader is the Leadership of James T. Kirk, captain of the USS Enterprise (Fig. 7.5). Throughout the whole series of Star Trek (Roddenberry 1966–1969), he is fully accepted as a Leader and captain, although (or maybe because?) he has his personal weaknesses and although (or maybe because?) these weaknesses regularly become visible and tangible.

The secret of his Leadership: James T. Kirk derives his strength from his team of officers around him, who represent a quite broad Diversity of Team

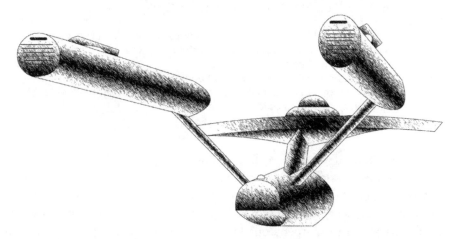

Fig. 7.5 The USS Enterprise of Captain James T. Kirk (source: www.pixabay.com, created by mdherren, amended)

(especially when we consider that this TV series was produced in the 1960s in the United States, at a time when there was still significant racial conflicts and even segregation in the United States).

The team of officers of James T. Kirk comprises Spock, a cold-blooded, logical, and analytical half Vulcan, half human, forming a perfect counterbalance to the sometimes quite emotional and illogically acting James T. Kirk. Other officers like the more caring and empathic Doctor McCoy and technology-minded expert Scott ("Scotty") compensate further weaknesses of James T. Kirk. Further characters, like the black communication officer Mrs. Uhura, the Japanese origin Sulu, and Russian officer Chekov add even more to the quite broad Diversity of Kirk's team.

Kirk as captain and Leader quite often uses the Diversity of his Team as a rich source of competences, of feedback, and of valuable second opinions on complex problems, in order to view things from various perspectives before taking a clear and often courageous decision. And very often, this is how an adventure of the USS Enterprise, where things really look bad or even hopeless—of course construed for the sake of movie thrill—is finally turned into a happy ending.

Exercise on Centricity

First think about your own Leadership situation, and look for an analogy, the picture of a Leader, to describe your own Leadership Role in a simple way, as you would describe it for a 5-year-old child.
Then ask yourself:
What is it that defines the characteristics of the Leader in my analogy, in my picture that I have chosen?
How does that understanding contribute to my personal Leadership situation, where does it give me clarity about my own position, my Role, my responsibilities and about those of the persons around me?
How can I strengthen my own Leadership behavior by consciously focusing on core characteristics of this Leadership picture, and make them visible and tangible for my Team and other people around me?

When you have developed such a Leadership picture for yourself, and answered these questions for yourself, please feel free to discuss the result also with your direct Leader. He or she may appreciate this discussion, and of course, he or she is one of the main persons in your direct environment to give you feedback and to sharpen your Leadership understanding even more. In addition he or she will—of course—have own expectations of you, how you should act and perform as a Leader, so you better cross-check these expectations with your direct Leader. The picture and the answers you have developed for yourself may make such a cross-check of expectations much easier.

Conclusion for Your Leadership

When talking about Habits, it is not about a singular action or a one-time behavior. It is about a general way of acting, about how we "use to do things."

It is about Role behavior.

As a Leader, we usually—consciously or unconsciously—live a certain Role, depending on the specific situation. We cannot avoid it. It is important to actively deal with your own Role and—literally—to develop a clear picture of your own Role for yourself, for your Self. The more you are aware of your current Role, the picture of your Role, your understanding of your own Role and your current role behavior, and the more you live it with full consciousness, the more you will *BE* this Role.

It is important that this picture of your Role arise from your own inner (self)understanding. By truly finding your understanding of the Role (or several Roles) and habits that really correspond to "yourself—your Self" and by literally visualizing yourselves at the Center of that Role, you can have a powerful impact on the people around you without "tumbling around."

References

Belbin RM (1993) Team roles at work. Routledge, New York

Blanchard K, Onken W (2000) The one minute manager meets the monkey. HarperCollins, London

García H, Miralles F (2017) Ikigai – The Japanese secret to a long and happy life. Random House, New York

Lucas G (director) (1977) Star wars episode IV – a new hope

Meier U (2010) Du bist die Entscheidung – schnell und entschlossen handeln. S. Fischer, Frankfurt a.M.

Moestl B (2011) Die 13 Siegel der Macht – Von der Kunst der guten Führung. Knaur, München

Moestl B (2016) Denken wie ein Shaolin – Die sieben Prinzipien emotionaler Selbstbestimmung, Knaur, München

Pink D, RSA Animate (2010) The surprising truth about what motivates us. YouTube. https://www.youtube.com/watch?v=u6XAPnuFjJc. Accessed May 22, 2018

Roddenberry G (director) (1966–1969). Star Trek. TV series

Sprenger RK (2008) Gut aufgestellt – Fußballstrategien für Manager. Campus, Frankfurt a.M.

Wachtel S (2014) Sei nicht authentisch – warum klug manchmal besser ist als echt. Plassen, Kulmbach

Wachtel S (2017) Executive Modus – 12 Taktiken für mehr Führungswirkung. Hanser, München

Wikipedia (2018) Gewohnheit. Wikipedia Die freie Enzyklopädie. https://de.wikipedia.org/wiki/Gewohnheit. Accessed May 22, 2018

8

Via Actions to Centricity

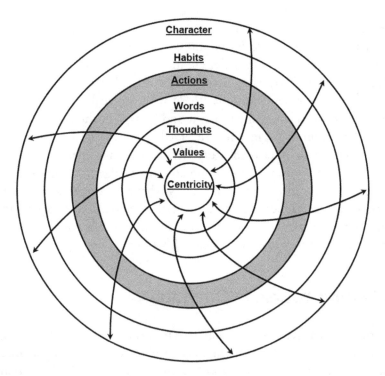

Actions (source: own drawing)

Actions are something that we consciously do in a targeted manner, that we can control and do with purpose, according to our motives. Everything that we do consciously and can control, we can of course use to work on our Focus and our Centricity. Via human evolution, we have developed a character and

T. H. Ulrich, *Spiritual Leadership*, https://doi.org/10.1007/978-3-030-45432-6_8

mindset for which it is very helpful and instructive to build on experiences and to make conscious experiences based on physical action, on Actions. Focus and Centricity in Action can help us to improve our Leadership, because Leadership means, on the one hand, learning to focus on essential things. On the other hand, an Awareness of practical ways to focus and, in particular, to use our inner (energy) Center helps us to develop an inner strength that also strengthens our Leadership and its perception by others.

Let us first have a look at a definition of the term "Action" in an encyclopedia:

Action means any human, purposeful activity guided by motives, be it active doing or omission. (translated from Wikipedia 2018a)

This means that Actions are something which we consciously do and can control, and which we do with purpose. Everything we do consciously and can control, we can of course use to work on our Focus and our Centricity.

You may ask: Why should Focus and Centricity derived from Actions help us to improve our Leadership? After all, most of us are not "manual workers," but "brain workers." My chemistry teacher in high school always said: "to understand, to grasp something has to do with physically 'grasping' it." This means: (only) if you can really touch it and "grasp" it, then you fully understand it. Christopher Klein and Jens Helbig (2017) also explain in their book—which I will discuss in more detail in a later chapter—that we as human beings often draw our learning and knowledge from physical experience. In the course of human evolution, we have developed a character and mindset for which it is very helpful and instructive to build on experience and to consciously experience based on physical action, on Actions.

One first aspect to work on Actions is how we "act on stage."

Positioning Yourself "On Stage"

Let us start with a situation you may face in business life as well as in private life, a situation where it becomes literally visible to everybody if you are aware of your Center, our Centricity, and are using it consciously. It is about the question: Where should you position yourself when you are "on stage"? Here, "on stage" can literally mean on a stage, where you do a presentation or a speech.

Ask yourself, or even better, observe yourself: does it happen to you that, when you are "on stage," you find yourself positioned at the side of the stage, offside a presentation screen, in a corner, where you feel safe, even like kind of "hiding" from the audience, as shown in Fig. 8.1?

If you become aware of this, then try to observe consciously what happens: the audience will mainly focus on the presentation, to what happens on the screen,

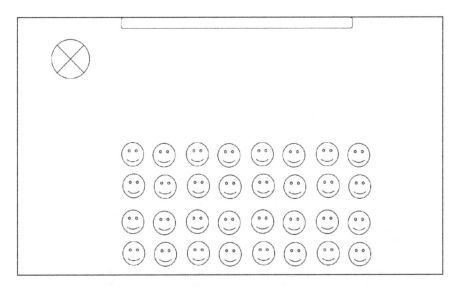

Fig. 8.1 Acting on Stage—offside (source: own drawing)

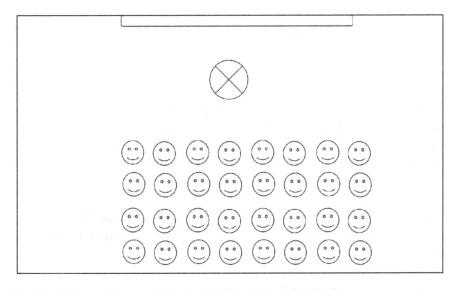

Fig. 8.2 Acting on Stage—in the Center (source: own drawing)

trying to capture the text and visuals there; however, you as a person will not get any visibility. Your words may even get overheard. Your impact on the audience will be significantly reduced. Simply because you are not "in the Center."

However, this is easy to change, if you take a little bit of courage. Just try. Position yourself into the direct line of sight of your audience, in the middle of the stage, as shown in Fig. 8.2. Find your Center on the stage; *BE* the stage, it is *YOUR* stage.

Exercise on Centricity

When you are "on stage" for the next time, try to consciously practice the following steps:

- Take your time before you start your presentation; observe if and how your audience will focus on you.
- Wait until you are in their focus, until you can feel you are "in the Center." Even if this moment of silence on stage may feel long for you.
- Take this moment for yourself to center yourself, to find Centricity for yourself, for your Self.
- Calm down your breath to conscious and slow breathing.
- And only then start to speak. Focus on your words; pronounce them slowly and loud. Try to force yourself to speak slower than you usually do, against the impulse of your natural nervousness, which wants to push you to speed up, in order to escape as soon as possible from the stressful situation.
- Look your audience into the eyes; keep the eye contact and attract the attention, the Awareness of your audience onto you.
- Lead your audience through your speech with a Focus on your main messages, using only some, but well selected core visuals as a support to your presentation.

Then observe and feel what this Centricity on stage does to your posture, to your speech, and to the impact you have on the audience.

Let us now move away from business environment to private life, as there are many situations in private life in which you can also work on and practice Focus and Centricity. You may ask yourself: why and how could that contribute to my Leadership? The answer is simple: because Leadership is always about yourself, about your Self. You can work on your Self in anything you do, in any practice, in any activity in your life.

This is known since long from Asian philosophy, as Shissai Chozuan wrote in "Tengu-Geijutsu-Ron—Discourse on the Art of the Mountain Demons" (on the true principle of sword art):

The heart is like a clear mirror or calm water. As soon as consciousness and thinking disturb the heart in the slightest, its clarity is impaired and it cannot develop freely. Today's artists do not know what it means to be free and unimpeded in one's reactions out of the stillness of the heart. They use tricks of consciousness, wear out their minds on nonessential things, and believe that they can achieve mastery that way, all on their own.

For this reason, they equally fail to achieve anything in other arts. There are many arts, and if you wanted to practice each one, one life would not be enough to master them. If, however, you let your heart completely melt in one single art, then you will also know about the other arts, even without having any practical experience in them. (translated from: Chozuan 1728)

In his book "The Art of Leadership" (Zapke-Schauer 2003), Gerhard Zapke-Schauer points out that Leadership is also an art that you can at least partially learn, but that also requires specific skills which are based on your personal Character and which you cannot learn. We already heard about getting to know the own Character in a previous chapter.

I already mentioned the book "Ikigai—The Japanese Secret to a Long and Happy Life" of Héctor García and Francesc Miralles (2017) in the previous chapter. Therein, the authors explain a Japanese concept and understanding of the importance to find for yourself your very personal Ikigai (生き甲斐) which means "a reason for being," to perceive it and to focus on it, to put it at the Center of your own life and being. It can be a deep professional vocation or an art that you can focus on throughout the course of your life, so that it can become a rich source of passion and give your life sense and meaning, as your life can be arranged around, can move around this core sense and meaning at the Center of your being.

Acting "On Stage": Dancing

I will start with the Activity of Dancing (see Fig. 8.3), as a still—or recently again—quite popular activity as a hobby in private life, and which I am practicing myself since more than 30 years, because every dance floor is of course also a kind of stage.

Dances, especially ballroom dances, have developed over many years and are usually designed and meant in a way that a couple is dancing together. That sounds logic. So where is the problem? Maybe you have also seen and felt that sometimes the dancers of a dancing couple are dancing sophisticated figures and moves, but not really "dancing together," in a sense that each of them is rather dancing and moving more or less for himself/herself. Watching such a couple, you can maybe even recognize that the looks of the dancers wander around in the room while dancing, to check if the others around are watching, either to seek admiration if the dancer(s) think they are good, or to check if somebody makes jokes about them if the dancer(s) feel uncomfortable. You may even perceive that the one dancing partner rather uses the other as a "decoration" or as kind of "amplifying tool" to make himself or herself look even more professional and high-class dancer.

Fig. 8.3 Centricity in dancing (source: own photo)

However, the ideal way of dancing as a couple is that the movements of the couple are kind of "melting together" and forming "one unity," the couple becoming like one body, centered around a common axis, both in movement and in attentiveness, in Awareness, both moving around a common Center of gravity.

It is interesting that in the essay of Heinrich von Kleist "On the Marionette Theatre," there is already a very distinct description about Centricity in dancing:

Each movement ... has its center of gravity; it is enough to control this within the puppet. The limbs, which are only pendulums, then follow mechanically of their own accord, without further help.

The advantage puppets would have over living dancers ... first of all a negative one: it would never be guilty of affectation. For affectation is seen ... when the soul, or moving force, appears at some point other than the center of gravity of the movement.

So grace itself returns when knowledge has as it were gone through an infinity. Grace appears most purely in that human form which either has no consciousness or an infinite consciousness. That is, in the puppet or in the God. (Kleist 1810, translated)

Exercise on Centricity

You can try yourself the following if you too are a dancer actively practicing Dancing:

- Focus only on your dancing partner. Try to close your eyes from time to time.
- If you are short sighted, take off your glasses, to avoid your Focus to drift away from your common movement as a dancing couple.
- Observe if you can experience a change in your movements, in how it feels to dance *together*, to dance *jointly as one.*
- If it in fact starts to feel different, then you have probably developed a feeling for Centricity.

Acting "On Stage": Asian Martial Arts

There are some Asian Martial Arts (Fig. 8.4) that nowadays are trained and practiced in a very practical way, be it for competitions—such as championships—or for practical self-defense use, and which—at least in the western world—are rather seen as sports than as arts:

Karate-dō, Judō, Kendō, Kung Fu (Chinese 功夫 Gōngfū), Tae Kwon Do, and Muay Thai are just a few of them to be named.

In recent years, such Martial Arts have even been combined with fitness training programs, which have given rise to new "styles" such as Tae Bo, Fit Boxing, etc., and which are now competing with other workout styles such as aerobics, Zumba, etc. However, their goal is clearly purely sports and fitness workout; you will not find any philosophy in it. Do not get me wrong, I do not want to speak badly of such workout styles, as I myself still really appreciate such good fitness training, because each one of us—especially as a Leader—should definitely pay attention to the own physical fitness. There is good reason that nowadays many companies offer health checks and health programs for managers as well as for employees.

Fig. 8.4 Asian Martial Arts (source: own photo)

However, in this book I would like to focus on the more traditional side or sphere of Martial Arts, a sphere that is strongly interconnected with a corresponding philosophy, permeated by it. This sphere can still be found in specific Martial Arts today, especially in those Martial Arts that are practiced without an opponent, without counterpart, so that—by their nature of practice—already require a higher degree of "abstraction." Such kind of Martial Arts are Iaidō (Japanese 居合道, the art of sword drawing), Kyudō (Japanese 弓道, the art and the way of Japanese archery), and Tai Chi Chuan (Chinese 太极拳 Tàijíquán). However, also in Martial Arts that are practiced with a counterpart or opponent, you can find (again)—increasingly in recent years—the traditional philosophies of Martial Arts, based on some trends to return to old, traditional values, and the roots of such arts.

The importance of the interconnection between Martial Arts and philosophy is also visible from the fact that the names of the Japanese Martial Arts end with the syllable "Dō" (Japanese: 道). This syllable is the Japanese word for "way." Because originally these Martial Arts were understood as a lifelong way of physical and mental learning and personal development, just the same as other Japanese arts, such as Chadō (the tea way = tea ceremony) or Shodō (the way of writing = calligraphy). I will come back to the art of Shodō in a later chapter.

In the following, I would like to describe some examples of Martial Arts and their importance for Focus and Centricity. I would also like to mention some books that deal with a linkage between Martial Arts and Leadership, namely the books of Robert Pater "LEADING from WITHIN" (Pater 1988), of Jutta Schanze and Jürgen Schuster "Der Weg zur Meisterschaft in der Führung" (Schanze and Schuster 2014) and of Jürgen Gottschalck and Alfons Heinz-Trossen "Qi-Management—Die Kata der Manager" (Gottschalck and Heinz-Trossen 2014).

Karate

I am practicing Karate (or more exactly: Karate-Dō, Japanese空手道, see Fig. 8.5) since more than 20 years now. In Karate we practice so-called Kata forms, having a clearly defined sequence of defensive techniques and blocks and offensive (counter)attacks of punches and kicks, the most powerful of them being even more amplified by a loud "Kiai" shout or yell (Japanese: 気合, where Ki 気 means "energy").

Very instructive graphic representations of katas can be found in Albrecht Pflüger's highly recommended book "25 Shotokan-Katas" (Pflüger 1995), which I have been using for many years to prepare for kata training and kata practice. This book contains low-level katas as well as high-level katas, such as the katas "Bassai Dai" and "Jion," which I had to present in my own black belt Karate grading examination in 2010 to achieve the so-called "first Dan" (first black belt rank).

As said, the sequence of a Kata is a clearly defined, fixed sequence of defensive defense techniques and offensive (counter) attacks with punches and kicks. Figure 8.6 shows a schematic and simplified representation of how a Kata looks like and how it is usually depicted.

A Kata can be a fairly long sequence of more or less complex movements and turns, involving attacking as well as defending techniques. At first glance, it appears quite simple to do: you just imitate, just copy the movements and positions as shown to you by your trainer, or even from the drawings in a

Fig. 8.5 Karate (source: own photo)

book only, and everything is fine. However, the danger that lies in such an approach to Karate Katas is: you easily get "stuck" in focusing solely on the techniques. The risk of focusing only on the process or the sequence, i.e., on the "superficial, outer" truth and formal correctness of the Kata, instead of focusing on the deeper meaning of each technique, i.e., on the inner meaning and on a true understanding of the meaning of the Kata.

However, Gichin Funakoshi—the founder of modern karate—already pointed out in his book "Karate-Dō—My Way of Life" (Funakoshi 1975) in his "six rules" of Karate, how essential it is not just to practice the sequence of a Kata. How essential it is to gain an understanding of the meaning of the Kata, and how important it is to train and to practice with your heart and soul, not just with your body.

However, what changes when you consciously focus on such meaning, such purpose, and "soul" of the Kata? When you start by first getting a clear understanding of what each Action, each technique means, what the imaginary situation is that the Kata represents, and when you next continue by visualizing this situation in your mind, centering your mind on that understanding and visualization, and only *THEN* finally start doing the Kata sequence? You will experience the following: All you do in the Kata becomes more distinct, more powerful and more "real," more authentic, much more centric.

When you focus on your inner Center during the Kata, and when you try to eliminate everything else that distracts the Focus; when you focus on what

Fig. 8.6 Karate Kata, schematic and simplified depiction (source: http://www.pixabay.com, created by Clker-Free-Vector-Images, amended)

each Action, each movement "really means;" when you visualize in your mind what each block, each punch, each kick is supposed to do; when you also visualize your counterparts, the opponents in your mind who are "dancing" through the Kata with you; then the Kata gets "real," each Action, each movement gets a true sense, and you yourself, your Self will feel completely Centered, will develop an inner axis of Centricity, while your arms, hands, legs, and the virtual opponents keep moving around this axis of Centricity.

At this point I would like to take up two essential points of the philosophy of Asian Martial Arts, which we will encounter some more times in the following: the essence of breathing and the "energy center" of the body (Japanese: "Hara"—腹 or Chinese "lower Dantian" 下 丹田—Xià Dāntián, see Fig. 8.7).

Let us start with the energy center "Hara": Hara literally means "belly" (you may be familiar with the term "Hara-Kiri," literally "belly cutting," a term for the ritual suicide of the samurai). In Asian philosophy, Hara also describes the energetic center of the body, the Focus of the human body, the starting point of inner energy. According to Asian philosophy, the energy "feeding" body, mind, and soul arises from the Hara, the energy center. A detailed description of this philosophy can be found in Karlfried Graf Dürckheim's book "Hara: The Vital Center of Man" (Dürckheim 2004).

Now let us focus on breathing: The energetic effect of the Hara is closely linked to breathing, if breathing is practiced as "right breathing," starting from the abdominal area. We will learn more about this in the following sections. The Kiai shout just mentioned before is not (just) a martial scream that

Fig. 8.7 The energy center Hara (source: http://www.pixabay.com, created by mohamed_hassan, amended)

accompanies an attack technique to additionally intimidate the (virtual, imaginary) opponent. Rather, the Kiai is a rapid, explosive exhalation, which gives the attack technique a particularly strong push of energy, which ultimately arises from the energy center, the Hara, and which is passed on to the attack technique (fist, elbow, foot). As said, Kiai comprises the syllable Ki = energy, which is combined with the syllable Ai = coming together or harmony. Kiai therefore describes a way of harmoniously bundling physical and mental energy at the moment of striking or kicking.

In the next sections and chapters, we will learn more about the importance of the human energy center and the influence of breathing.

Tai Chi Chuan

Tai Chi Chuan (Chinese 太极拳 Tàijíquán, short: Tai Chi, see Figs. 8.8 and 8.9) is often underestimated and sometimes smiled at as a "sport for elderly people," in my experience not only in the West, but also in China itself ("only old people do that"). I have done so, too, for many years, because for a

Fig. 8.8 Tai Chi Chuan (source: own photo)

Fig. 8.9 Tai Chi Chuan practice (source: own photo)

"dynamic youngster Karateka" the movements of Tai Chi actually look comparatively "weak" at first glance. (It is probably the same reaction that many people have with respect to yoga when they see it for the first time; not practicing by themselves, they may assume "it is all very easy and relaxed"—which of course every yoga practitioner would strongly deny.)

However, in the meantime I have realized from my own experience that Tai Chi is a very valuable practice—not only in addition to other martial arts, but also as an art on its own, as a spiritual art. For a better understanding, I recommend you the book of Linda Myoki Lehrhaupt "T'ai Chi as a Path of Wisdom" in which she does not only describe how to practice Tai Chi, but also shares a very personal view on Tai Chi, including practical exercises (Lehrhaupt 2013). Tai Chi is a martial art in itself; it is just practiced more slowly than other martial arts. This is precisely where (true) Tai Chi practice becomes valuable: only if you learn to sense, to feel your Focus, to center yourself, to find your inner Center, to sense the Focus of a movement, and to focus on the meaning and on the execution of every movement, only then will you be able to practice a stable and fluent Tai Chi without "tumbling."

Another element of Tai Chi is to feel and work with the "energy" in the inner Center of the body, especially with the previously mentioned energy center, which in Chinese is called "lower Dantian" (下 丹田—Xià Dāntián), and which, according to Asian understanding, is located about three fingers wide below the navel and two fingers wide inside the body. In Asia, this energy center is regarded as the "source of life and energy" in our body. Tai Chi ideally "happens" around this point of maximum physical inner Centricity in our body, the arms and legs move as if they were

"…only pendulums, following mechanically of their own accord, without further help…,"

while the body and mind are centered in this energy center. This description may remind you of the passage from Heinrich von Kleist's "About the Marionette Theater" already quoted above, and rightly so. When you watch closely, you can notice a good and true Tai Chi practitioner, as his movements all start from his "Center of gravity," from the Center of his body. If Tai Chi is practiced in a way that

"…the soul, or moving force, appears at some point other than the center of gravity of the movement…,"

then Tai Chi becomes "hollow."

I saw a documentary program about Tai Chi many years ago, and in this documentary, the Tai Chi master gave his students the following task: "Try doing Tai Chi while focusing on the dirt under your fingernails." Then he did a few Tai Chi movements as an example, constantly looking at his fingernails. The whole audience laughed aloud, because it looked completely ridiculous. Only much later I understood what he was actually talking about: he was talking about the inner Center, about inner Centricity as the basis for Tai Chi.

You can try for yourself, even if you are not actively practicing Tai Chi. Just try doing some tai chi-like movements while focusing on your fingernails: it will actually feel ridiculous and you will look ridiculous. Why? For the same reason Heinrich von Kleist writes about in his essay "About the Marionette Theater": If you focus on your fingernails, then "the soul," the Focus of the Action, of the movement lies outside your true Center of the Tai Chi practitioner. The "soul" of the Tai Chi "dancer" has moved from his inner Center to a spot under his fingernails: He has lost his Centricity.

Exercise on Centricity (Quite Similar to the Dancing Exercise)

If you practice Martial Arts like Karate or Tai Chi, or other similar Arts where the practice includes repeating predefined Actions, sequences, or movements, try the following while you practice:

- Before starting to practice, visualize in your mind every Action, every movement of the sequence.
- Visualize in your mind the Actions and movements of your (imaginary) counterpart in that Art.
- Close your eyes and perform your Actions, your movements, your training sequence "blind."
- As an alternative—if you are short sighted and if you prefer a safer feeling and more orientation in the room—simply take off your glasses
- To avoid your Focus to drift away from the true sense and deeper understanding of your Actions.

You will recognize that the movements are increasingly coming "from inside you, out of your inner Center." You may even feel an energy that arises from within, an energy flow that makes the movements more powerful, more energetic.

Kyūdō Archery and the Transition to Philosophy

You have most probably heard of Karate and Tai Chi, but you may be asking yourself: what is Kyūdō (Japanese 弓道, the art and the way of Japanese archery, see Fig. 8.10)? This would not really be a surprise, because in my experience Kyūdō is not widely known in the western world.

In the Wikipedia encyclopedia, we can find the following:

Kyūdō (Japanese, "way of the bow") is an art of Japanese archery practiced since the 16th century, which is characterized by its formal, slow movements.

…

From the 4th to the 9th century, the close contacts between China and Japan had a great influence on Japanese archery, especially the Confucian belief that archery can reveal a person's true Character.

…

In Kyūdō, Munenmuso or Mushin (which can be translated as "empty spirit") should be reached in full draw and when releasing the shot. However, this [Munenmuso] does not correspond to a general aimless indifference, but rather describes the state of such a high and condensed concentration that there is no room for other thoughts. (translated from Wikipedia 2018b)

Fig. 8.10 Kyūdō (source: www.pixabay.com, created by Sciengineer, amended)

This makes Kyūdō anything but a purely athletic or purely physical martial art. It is much more apt to see Kyūdō as a combination of martial arts movement and meditative philosophy, literally as the "way of the bow" in a sense of a lifelong way of personal—physical and, above all, spiritual—development. This is why people call Kyūdō a "Zen art," because in many aspects it corresponds to the philosophy of Zen. See, for example, Shunryu Suzuki's book "Zen Mind—Beginner's Mind" (Suzuki 2006, German publication: Suzuki 1975).

In order to get to know the essence of Japanese art of Kyūdō archery from a western point of view, I would like to refer to Eugen Herriegel's well-known book "Zen in der Kunst des Bogenschießens" (Herriegel 1999, English publication: "Zen in the Art of Archery," Herriegel 1989), which he wrote in the 1950s. His description of Kyūdō and his personal experiences when studying Kyūdō in Japan go far beyond the purely physical study of archery, and he very impressively describes the difficulties that he—as a western character—has in dealing with and getting an understanding for the essence, the deeper meaning of the Kyūdō.

Herriegel also describes how his Kyūdō master conveys to him the essence of Kyūdō, in particular the importance of "true breathing" from the Center, i.e., the (energy) center of the body:

> In order to unleash the full force of this spiritual awareness, you must perform the ceremony differently: rather as a good dancer dances. If you do this, your movements will spring from the Center, from the seat of right breathing. (Herriegel 1999, translated as Herriegel 1989; source: Copyright ©2010 O.W. Barth Verlag, ein Imprint der Verlagsgruppe Droemer Knaur GmbH & Co. KG, München.)

Maybe these words already seem familiar to you. That is right, because Herriegel refers to Heinrich von Kleist's "About the Marionette Theater," the text we heard about in previous sections. In fact, Herriegel explicitly refers to the analogy and understanding of the Center, i.e., to Centricity, as Kleist describes in the "Marionette Theater" in relation to dancing, although Kleist comes to this understanding from a different starting point. Besides that, it is interesting to note that even the famous author Paulo Coelho recently took up this topic, too, in his book "The Way of the Bow" (German publication: "Der Weg des Bogens," Coelho 2017).

This was actually a very important insight for myself from my own experience and my own learning in the 50 years of my life: It does not matter where you start from, no matter what you are dealing with, which actions, arts, or occupations you practice. If you do it carefully and if you try to sense a deeper, inner meaning, and energy, then you will inevitably develop an understanding of Centricity. As we learned at the beginning of this chapter from Shissai Chozuan's quote in "Tengu-Geijutsu-Ron—Discourse on the Art of Mountain Demons" (about the true principle of sword art):

> If, however, you let your heart completely melt in one single art, then you will also know about the other arts, even without having any practical experience in them. (translated from: Chozuan 1728)

The same way, Herriegel recognizes in his book that the aim, the true target of the archer is not the physical archery target (Fig. 8.11), but rather lies in the archer himself. It is the aim, in spite of his doing, his Actions, and yet with the help of his doing, his Actions, to reach an unmoved still core, an unmoved Center. The goal is to achieve Centricity:

> It is necessary for the archer to become, in spite of himself, an unmoved center. Then comes the supreme and ultimate miracle.

Fig. 8.11 The target of the archer (source: www.pixabay.com, created by OpenClipart-Vectors, amended)

art becomes "artless",
shooting becomes not-shooting,
a shooting without bow and arrow,
the teacher becomes a pupil again,
the Master a beginner,
the end a beginning
and the beginning perfection. (Herriegel 1999, translated as Herriegel 1989; source: Copyright © 2010 O.W. Barth Verlag. Ein Imprint der Verlagsgruppe Droemer Knaur GmbH & Co. KG, München.)

Thus, Kyūdō clearly is an art that lies between martial arts and philosophy, because the art of Kyūdō is the bridge that leads the archer to his ultimate target, to become an "unmoving Center," to achieve Centricity.

Therefore, also in Kyūdō—or particularly in Kyūdō—the following applies: If you focus on your inner Center, omit everything around that distracts the Focus, if you visualize your target in your mind rather than seeing it with your eyes, then every action, every movement becomes centric, becomes centered, and you will feel yourself, your Self to become completely centered. You will develop for yourself, for your Self an inner axis of Centricity, while your body, mind, and spirit move around this axis of Centricity.

Conclusion for Your Leadership

Actions are something that we consciously do in a targeted manner, so that we can control and do it with purpose. Everything that we do consciously and can control, we can of course use to work on our Focus and our Centricity.

Focus and Centricity in Actions can help us improve our Leadership, because successful Leadership means, learning to:

– Focus on the essentials
– Focus on our strengths

It does not matter where you start from, no matter what you are dealing with, which actions, arts, or occupations you practice. If you do it carefully and if you try to sense a deeper, inner meaning, and energy, then you will inevitably develop an understanding of Centricity. It is the aim, in spite of our doing, our Actions, and yet with the help of our doing, our Actions, to reach an unmoved still core, an unmoved Center.

If in your Actions you are already developing a feeling for centering yourself, and especially for using your inner (energy) Center, then you can develop an inner strength, energy, and power that can strengthen your Leadership and its perception by others.

References

Chozuan S, Tengu-Geijutsu-Ron – Diskurs über die Kunst der Bergdämonen (über das wahre Prinzip der Schwertkunst, 1728, e.g. in Kammer R (1993) ZEN in der Kunst, das Schwert zu führen, O.W. Barth Verlag, Frankfurt a.M
Coelho P (2017) Der weg des Bogens, Diogenes, Zürich
Dürckheim K (2004) Hara: The vital Center of Man. Inner Traditions, Rochester
Funakoshi G (1975) Karate-dō – my way of life. Kodansha International Ltd, Tokyo

García H, Miralles F (2017) Ikigai – The Japanese secret to a long and happy life. Random House, New York

Gottschalk J, Heinz-Trossen A (2014) Qi-Management – Die Kata der Manager. Springer Gabler, Berlin

Herriegel E (1989) Zen in the Art of Archery. Vintage Random House, New York

Herriegel E (1999) Zen in der Kunst des Bogenschießens. O.W. Barth, Frankfurt a.M

Klein C, Helbig J (2017) Meditation für Anfänger. GbR, Düsseldorf

Kleist Hv, Über das Marionettentheater, 1810, e.g. in Kleist Hv (2013) Über das Marionettentheater (Studienausgabe), Reclam, Ditzingen

Lehrhaupt L (2013) T'ai Chi as a Path of Wisdom. Shambala Publications, Boston

Pater R (1988) LEADING from WITHIN. Park Street Press, Rochester

Pflüger A (1995) 25 Shotokan-Kateas, Falken, Niederhausen

Schanze J, Schuster J (2014) Der Weg zur Meisterschaft in der Führung. Springer Gabler, Wiesbaden

Suzuki S (1975) Zen-Geist – Anfänger-Geist. Theseus, Zürich

Suzuki S (2006) Zen Mind – Beginner's Mind. Shambhala, Boston

Wikipedia (2018a) Handeln. Wikipedia Die freie Enzyklopädie. https://de.wikipedia.org/wiki/Handeln. Accessed May 22, 2018

Wikipedia (2018b) Kyūdō. Wikipedia Die freie Enzyklopädie. https://de.wikipedia.org/wiki/Kyudo. Accessed May 22, 2018

Zapke-Schauer G (2003) The Art of leadership. Gabler, Wiesbaden

9

Via Words to Centricity

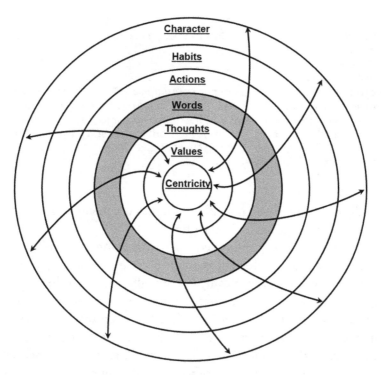

Words (Source: own drawing)

T. H. Ulrich, *Spiritual Leadership*, https://doi.org/10.1007/978-3-030-45432-6_9

If the words
  "Thank you"
  Were the only prayer
  That you ever speak
  It would be sufficient. (Meister Eckhart, 1260–1327)

This chapter is rather short. However, as often in life, the little things, the simple things can already have a big effect. Often it is not so easy to remember that we really should do those little things in life. This chapter is about the effect of Words. So easy to use, available for free, and always at your disposal.

Exercise on Centricity

In order to test how powerful words can be, I recommend you one very simple exercise you can try during one day:
Say "Thank you."
To everybody who does something for you.
Start with your family in the morning. Say "thank you" to your wife or husband who has prepared your breakfast. To your children who help you with something. To the person who brings you the newspaper, milk, or mail in the morning. To pedestrians or drivers on the way to work that let you pass by. To the man or woman that is emptying your wastepaper basket in the office, etc.
Then watch the effect of these simple two words.

I actually experienced this myself, so I on purpose mentioned the man who empties the wastepaper basket in the office:

In my case, it was a middle-aged man with a foreign, probably Indian appearance. I had just started my current job at our company in the Bosch Group, and every day that man came into my office at about the same time of the day, without mentioning a word, emptied the wastepaper basket into a small trolley, and disappeared again. When I realized that it was always the same man coming into my office every day, I started saying "thank you" to him and he started to smile. A few days later, when he came back into my office, I asked him: "We see each other every day, but I do not know your name. What is your name?" He stopped in the middle of the movement and said "Saïd, my name is Saïd." And gone he was again.

However, something had changed that day. When he came into my office from that day on, he would dash in, I greeted him with "Good morning, Mr. Saïd" and he replied, "Good morning, Mr. Ulrich." Then he emptied my wastepaper basket, I said "Thank you, and have a nice day, Mr. Saïd" and he dashed out smiling with a "Nice day to you, Mr. Ulrich."

In his book "Stell Dir vor, Du wachst auf—Die OOOO+X-Methode für mehr Präsenz und Klarheit" (Kurth 2018), Michael "Curse" Kurth describes an exercise of gratitude as a source of personal strength. It is not so much about thanking other people, but rather about an "inner" form of gratitude and thankfulness for what you experience yourself. It is about a feeling that unfolds from within your own body, form your inner Center, and that extends to your whole body like a positive energy.

Does that sound familiar to you? In the previous chapter, we had already dealt with the Hara, which is known in Asian philosophy since thousands of years and which—as already mentioned—also Karlfried Graf Dürckheim describes in his book "Hara: The Vital Center of Man" (Dürckheim 2004). Asian philosophy understands the Hara as an energy Center from which the energy for body, mind, and soul arises. Here it is now about the power of Words that arises from your inner Center. The quote by Meister Eckhardt, given as an example at the beginning of this chapter, shows that also in Western philosophy the meaning of seemingly simple yet powerful words and their positive energy were recognized already hundreds of years ago.

Thus, once again, the link—or even better the cycle, the circle—is closed again between modern literature and findings that have been known for centuries or even millennia from Eastern and Western philosophy. It is not without reason that the symbol of the circle has a special meaning in philosophy since a long time already (Fig. 9.1).

What can we learn from that?

Words have their own power, as through words—if carefully or carelessly selected—can strengthen or weaken our mind, our spirit, and our outward impact with respect to other persons around us. This applies both: to what we say—i.e., to the words we choose—as well as to how we speak.

Weak language like "I guess, I think, maybe we should" can make our mind, our spirit, our impact and ourselves weak. It makes us lose our Center, our stability, and our self-confidence. However, strong solid words can make our back straighten literally, give us a solid basis, and make our impact strong. Especially when we focus on expressing what we stand for, then we can do it with words that positively amplify our beliefs. We can be firm, clear, concise, strong, and can be in the Center of what we stand for.

Fig. 9.1 The circle in philosophy (source: http://www.pixabay.com, created by ArtsyBee, amended)

Exercise on Centricity

> Watch yourself like an outside observer the next time you are giving a speech or participate in a meeting or other types of discussion.
> Listen to your own words.
> If something like "I guess, I think, maybe we should" wants to come across your lips, stop these words or correct them and change them into strong, firm words, like:
> "I firmly believe that …, I am convinced that…, it is important that …".
> And watch the effect on the people around you.

Another way to use the power of words and the power of Centricity is the concept of qualified feedback. Yourself—and again, even more so your Self—as well as the persons around you, in your team as well as in your private life, can draw a lot from feedback if it is qualified feedback.

We are currently experiencing a corporate environment and management environment in which feedback is increasingly seen as an important issue. There are even training sessions for entire teams and departments to practice how to give each other feedback and accept feedback. In principle, I believe that is a positive development. However, the question arises as to when feedback is truly "valuable" feedback and when feedback becomes "hollow." Practical instructions for qualified feedback are already well known from literature; see for example the detailed description in great detail on the website www.karrierebiebel.de. I would like to lay out here the essential aspects for qualified feedback in the sense of Centricity.

Quite often we tend to say things like "nice," "I like it," or "good job!" and think we gave feedback. However, this is not the case. How should the person we are talking to know what was nice or good, and why we think it was nice or good, and how he can even improve more. This can only be achieved by qualified feedback, which also requires that we ourselves listen to our internal feedback and focus consciously on the things that we ourselves evaluate as positive. Therefore, we must first go to the Center of the behavior, of the Actions of the other person and then focus on our own Center and inner feedback to that behavior and Actions, and finally express is it in a qualified manner with Words that are clear, strong, and concise.

Exercise on Centricity

- Start to actively practice qualitative feedback with a person in your closer environment, a person that is "near" to you, be it in your team, in your private life or—if you like and dare—even a person you meet somewhere in the street,
- actively focus on expressing what exactly is the main, the core perception of what you find positive or negative.
- practice it by saying:
- "I perceive very positive/comforting/helpful that you do/say/act the following…, because by doing so, I perceive the following…,"
- or,
- "I perceive it disturbing/troubling/harmful that you do/say/act the following…, because by doing so, I perceive the following…,"
- And watch the effect it has on the other person and on yourself.

Ultimately, feedback is a method of determining a current position, determining one's own position. A method that helps you find your own Center, your own Centricity. We may say that position determination is a principle of "reverse Centricity analysis": it means using fixed positions—the Centricity—of other references in order to determine and cross-check your own current position, so to ultimately strengthen your own Centricity.

Methods of position determination are since long known from navigation. A classic method of determining the position in navigation is bearing:

This requires at least two references, the position and characteristics (the Character) of which are known and remain "stable."

Let us take ship navigation as an example: For many years—and still today—buoys have been used in ship navigation, which have a fixed position and individual characteristics (shape, color, type of light, duration of light, light sequence, sounds, etc.) and are precisely identified and labeled in the nautical charts (i.e., the maps of the seas). Of course, nowadays GPS navigation is usually used but the principle is the same: satellites, whose position and individual characteristics/signature are known and are the basis for determining one's own current position, are now used instead of buoys.

Figure 9.2 shows an example of a bearing in shipping using two buoys. One of them is a so-called safe water buoy or fairway buoy (also called "approach buoy"). In the example depicted in Fig. 9.2 it is named "ST," with the following characteristic: red and white (RW) vertical stripes, with a red ball at the top and with a common mode flashing light signal in white color (white light is shown in yellow color in nautical charts), having equally long, alternating

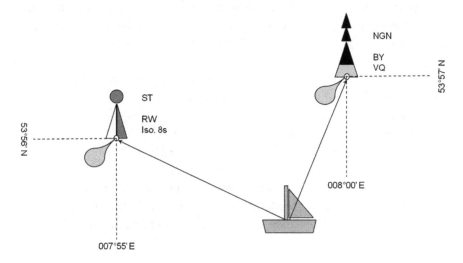

Fig. 9.2 Bearing in ship navigation (source: own drawing)

light and dark cycles with a repetition rate of 8 s (Iso.8 s). The second is a so-called "cardinal buoy," in Fig. 9.2 with the name NGN, which indicates an obstacle and has the defined characteristic black-yellow (BY) with two black cones at the top and a white light with a very quick sequence of successive flashes of light ("very quick" VQ). The respective position of the buoy is defined by the center of the buoy (the small circle in the middle at the bottom of the buoy), taking its exact longitude and latitude from the nautical charts. Everyone who has a boating license in Germany knows these buoys, as they frequently appear in boating license exam questions. See, for example, the book by Heinz Overschmidt and Axel Bark "Sportboot-Führerschein See" (Overschmidt and Bark 2017).

This means that to determine your own current position, you first have to get a very precise picture of where your selected reference "stands" with its Center and how the reference "is ticking," i.e., what is its characteristic, its Character (we have in a previous chapter has already dealt extensively with the importance of Character for Centricity).

The same applies to feedback: the better you know where someone stands (in a stable way!) and how he "is ticking," i.e., what his Character is, the more valuable his words are to you, the more valuable the feedback that you can get from this person, for your own position determination. Especially to get a feedback that is not "diffuse" or "hollow," but rather qualified feedback in a distinct context.

However, there is something to note when selecting human beings as a reference, in contrast to lifeless objects such as buoys: the phenomenon of interaction. A person's feedback is not objective, but there is an interaction between the observer person and the observed person, and this interaction also depends on what the observer focuses on in the observed person.

Modern physics is also familiar with this phenomenon; it is known in physics as the "Heisenberg uncertainty principle" and it is particularly relevant in particle physics (quantum physics), i.e., in the physics of elementary particles that are the basic structural parts of the entire universe, everything around us, including ourselves. The essence of the Heisenberg uncertainty principle: the more precisely an observer wants to observe and determine the location, the position of a particle, the less precise becomes the knowledge about the movement (in physics: the momentum) of this particle at the same time. The observer can never determine the position and movement of the particle at the same time with the same accuracy. Physics even go so far that the fact that an observer determines the position of the particle has an influence (interaction) on the movement of the particle. An explanation of these laws of physics can be found in any higher level standard book of physics, for example in "Gerthsen Physik" (currently already in its 25th edition: Meschede 2015).

In day-to-day Leadership, this is comparable to feedback discussions that a Leader may have with a team member: the Leader intends to give the team member helpful feedback to enable him to determine his or her current position in the team. However, if the Leader does not act carefully, then the team member may increasingly lose his (inner) balance, may start to "shift," to "rotate" and "tumble," precisely because of this situation of mutual interaction. That way, "bad" feedback can turn into a situation of less constructive or even destructive feedback. Conversely, positive feedback can also positively influence a certain positioning or movement.

Another principle of modern physics is also relevant in day-to-day Leadership: the principle of the theory of (special) relativity, developed by Albert Einstein. One principle of this theory is shown Fig. 9.3.

An observer A, being in his own reference system, cannot determine in which of the following situations he currently is:

Situation (a):

Whether an observed other individual B, who is in his own reference system, is moving constantly and uniformly relative to observer A, and whether observer A himself is "unmoved" (that is to say centered),

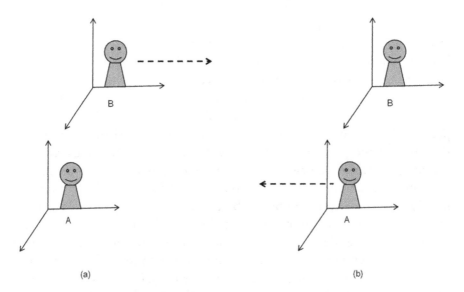

(a)   (b)

Fig. 9.3 Theory of special relativity: Reference systems in relative motion with respect to each other (source: own drawing)

or

Situation (b):

Whether the observer A himself is moving relative to the observed individual
B—but into the opposite direction—i.e., that observer A moves constantly
and uniformly relative to the reference system of observed individual B and
that the observed B is unmoved, i.e., centered.

Here a classical example for clarification:

You may know this situation when two trains are standing side by side in
the station. When one of the trains starts moving very slowly and smoothly
while you look out of the window, you can often not distinguish whether it is
your own train that is starting to move and the train opposite to you is at rest,
or if you yourself are at rest and the other train is moving. Each of two observers in the two opposite trains can rightly assume—from his subjective personal perception—that he is "at rest," is centered, while the other one, the
other observer, is the moving one (You may also know that from a "wrong-
way driver experience," in literal or figurative sense, when someone asks himself: "am I the wrong-way driver who is traveling in the wrong direction or is
it the other(s)?"). However, (at least in physic) both observers are somehow
right, because the theory of relativity no longer provides for an absolute reference system, for an "absolute truth" in case of such observations, but rather
for "relative truths" of both, the observer and the observed.

However, there are still situations under the theory of special relativity in
which the status of each of the two reference systems can be distinguished
from each other. Namely, when the observed reference system B does not
move constantly and uniformly, but rather is subject to a significant change in
the motion (in terms of physics: positive or negative acceleration), i.e., if
either the motion accelerates or slows down, or the respective observed system
rotates or "tumbles." To put it simple: if one of the systems is subject to forces
that influence or even impair it, then you can very well determine and observe
such influence, because these forces have a visible and tangible impact on the
corresponding system. Another system that rests (centered in itself) does not
show these effects. Thus, an unmoved (self-centered) system, an unmoved
(self-centered) observer can very well give feedback to another system or
observed person whether the observed person is also perceived unmoved and
self-centered, or whether the observed person shows recognizable impacts and
influence of forces that are changing the situation of the observed, that may
even cause him to "tumble."

Conclusion for Your Leadership

Words can be very powerful. We do well to choose our words carefully, to work consciously on what we say and how we say it. Because even a single word—depending on the situation—can have a great impact. It is up to us, our careful handling of our words, whether this effect will go in a positive or a negative direction, whether it will strengthen or weaken our Leadership.

A particular form of using words in Leadership is feedback. Feedback is never detached from the respective situation of observation, from the Focus of the observer, and can never be complete and objective. From the observation and the feedback situation itself results an interaction with respect to the observed person i.e., an interdependency between the observation and feedback given and its effect on the observed person. This means that, as Leaders, we should be very careful with feedback and be aware of these natural interactions and ambiguities, both when we give feedback and when we receive feedback. Because an "absolute truth" cannot exist by nature, but only relative truths. We have to live and accept this situation, both as a Leader as well as a colleague in a team, just as science had to say goodbye to the idea of an absolute truth and a comprehensive (pre)determinability of nature.

References

Dürckheim K (2004) Hara: The vital Center of Man. Inner Traditions, Rochester
Kurth M (2018) Stell Dir vor, Du wachst auf – Die OOOO+X-Methode für mehr Präsenz und Klarheit. Rowolth, Reinbek bei Hamburg
Meschede D (2015) Gerthsen Physik. Springer, Heidelberg
Overschmidt H, Bark A (2017) Sportboot-Führerschein See. Delius Klasing, Bielefeld
Website (2018) www.karrierebibel.de/feedback-geben

10

Via Thoughts to Centricity: Awareness

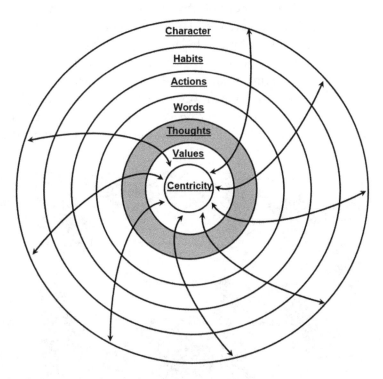

Thoughts (source: own drawing)

While walking and standing,
while sitting and lying,
when speaking and silent,
when having tea and having rice,

you must never stop your efforts;
you must focus immediately
at the target,
and explore the coming and going
deep down to the ground.
That way you have to gain direct insight into all things.
(Sōhō, approx. 1600, translated)

What Is Awareness?

What Takuan Sōhō (1573–1645) described in the above cited text of "Taiaki—Annals of the Sword Taia" already as early as the seventeenth century, is what we understand today when we speak of "Awareness." Here, too, the circle closes again between insights that have been known for centuries or millennia from Eastern and Western philosophy, and today's insights, which we are rediscovering and re-embracing in modern Leadership theory. I would like to illustrate a few examples of what the understanding of Awareness means for us today.

How many times does it happen to you that you try to "multiplex" your Thoughts: the TV is on during your breakfast or dinner, while at the same time you are checking the latest messages on your smartphone (Fig. 10.1) and

Fig. 10.1   Awareness in the world of connectivity and multimedia (source: own photo)

trying to have a talk with your wife, husband, or children? How many times do you drive to the office in your car and the business news radio channel is on while you already think about the tasks you have to do in the office today. Does that sound familiar to you?

How many times has it happened to you that—on the way to the office in your car, while listening to your preferred news radio channel—you already got worried or upset in the early morning? Maybe because of the latest news, maybe about the stock market going down again, maybe about a severe accident, a storm or even a war that has just happened, or maybe just because of some upsetting words or actions of a certain politician or of a certain president. Finally, you arrive in the office, already in pretty bad mood. What a day may lie ahead of you? Does that also sound familiar?

On the other hand, did it also happen that you switched the radio channel to one of the music stations—of course after getting an update on the essential news that a global manager should be aware of—and became aware that they just started to play one of your favorite songs, and all of a sudden you found yourself singing along loud in your car? What was the effect when you arrived in the office on that day? Maybe you even noticed that you kept singing or whistling this song for the whole daylong.

In their already mentioned book "Shaolin—Das Geheimnis der inneren Stärke" (Späth and Bao 2011), Dr. Thomas Späth and Shi Yan Bao deal intensively with human thinking, with the question how Thoughts arise and how we can work on them, how we can even control and generate positive Thoughts and feelings (remember the "two-finger smile" mentioned at the beginning) and how—ultimately—we can free ourselves from disturbing Thoughts. They derive from Asian philosophy of the Shaolin monks that we are indeed—or at least can become—masters of our Thoughts, can lead and guide them by focusing our Awareness on them.

So what does that teach us? It teaches us that our Thoughts have a great impact on ourselves, on our Self, but we ourselves, our Self also have influence on our Thoughts. A chaos in our Thoughts leaves us "tumbling around," leaving us without any deeper Awareness of the current situation around us and without real Awareness with respect to the persons around us, their needs and what keeps their minds busy or of what concerns them.

However, it is exactly this understanding, this competence—Awareness—that has a big impact on our Leadership, as the persons we work with, the persons around us—like all human beings worldwide—are quite sensitive to the presence or lack of Awareness. To work on a clear Focus on Awareness helps us to establish a Centricity in our Thoughts, in our Self—and this has nothing to do with being selfish, on the contrary. Centricity in Thoughts in the sense as laid out here is a source from which Awareness will just naturally emerge.

In that sense, "Awareness" is something that becomes clear in our impact, our focus *on everything around us*. When Awareness is there—it becomes tangible and can be perceived by the people around us. I will deal later with the effect our *Focus toward our inner core*, which we call "*Mindfulness*."

Exercise on Centricity

Use a reminder to remind yourself of Awareness. In previous chapters, I had already laid out possible reminders (such as a Totem) to remind yourself of things that are essential for you.
When using such reminder, you recognize that just right then you are in a situation where you ask yourself:
For the last 5 min

- What was said on the TV/radio?
- What did my wife, husband, or child just tell me?
- What did my breakfast, tea, or coffee taste like that I just had?
- What did the trees and houses besides the road look like that I was just driving by?

If there is at least one of the questions you cannot answer, then:

Reduce!

This means:
Consciously decide what you want to focus on,
center your thoughts and Awareness on it.
and
turn off the rest as much as possible.
(Yes, some things have an "off switch" that you can use consciously exactly for that purpose!)

Späth and Bao call this the "art of omission" (Späth and Bao 2011). Shunryu Suzuki explains in his already mentioned book "Zen Mind—Beginner's Mind" (Suzuki 2006) how we can deal with the "weeds of mind" in order to finally turn them into valuable Thoughts, into spiritual nourishment. In her book "Clear your clutter with Feng Shui" (Kingston 2016; corresponding German publication: "Feng Shui gegen das Gerümpel des Alltags," Kingsto 2003), Karen Kingston describes how important it is not only to get rid of the clutter that is a burden in our (physical) homes, but also of the "mental clutter" in our minds as the home of our thinking, of our Thoughts. And is not it true that we know from our own experience what happens when we burden ourselves with superfluous things, with clutter: This clutter acts like an inert mass that takes away our momentum, that makes our lives "imbalanced," brings us out of balance, out of our Center, and makes us "tumble."

However, it does not have to be like this. We do not have to allow that this happen. Because it is *your* decision what you want to focus on. There is nothing negative about listening to the radio in your car. You can even "sing and dance" if you like. For this, put your business thoughts aside for a while. If you want to have a good conversation with your wife, your husband, your children? Then put the smartphone away and turn off the TV. Modern technology gets in our way very easily, gets in our way where there should actually be a Focus on Awareness in our life (as we can see from a classical real-life example in Fig. 10.1).

Michael "Curse" Kurth advises in his book "Stell Dir vor, Du wachst auf— Die OOOO+X-Methode für mehr Präsenz und Klarheit" (Kurth 2018) that we should start our day without switching on the smartphone right away, in order to create a (spiritual) space for ourselves. A space in which we can focus our Thoughts on positive, valuable things instead of burdening ourselves with—all too often less valuable—Thoughts of other people. This knowledge is also likely to be very familiar to many parents, and likely to trigger some discussions in families at the breakfast table, namely when parents have to remind their children that there is still a real world beyond the virtual world of online communities and social media. However, as Kurth correctly points out, we also have to take a good look at ourselves regularly and remind ourselves of this principle.

I just described that it can be helpful to use a "reminder" to remind yourself of Awareness. As I already mentioned in the beginning of this book, I took the Habit of wearing a Buddhist Mala (i.e. Buddhist prayer beads) as a bracelet since quite a long time. As said, I first did so without being fully aware of what it really means for me, even when people asked me about it. I just felt it was important for me. Now I am wearing it with full consciousness, as it reminds me of what Buddhist way of life stands for—although I would not call myself a religious Buddhist. It is more a Symbol of Awareness and the way of how to treat other human beings. Wearing it calls this understanding back to my conscience and into my Focus.

You can of course use also other kinds of "reminders." Be it a rosary, an Islamic Tasbih prayer beads, such as the ones you can often see in Turkey (many men carry them with themselves)—or its toy-like brothers which you can find a lot in Greece, which are called Komboloi. Any other object or "toy" can also do, if it has a personal meaning for yourself. Be it, for example, things like Baoding balls—also called Qi balls or Qigong balls (Chinese: 保定健身球—Bǎodìng Jiànshēn Qiú). Even one of the recently very popular fidget spinner toys can do (Fig. 10.2). In fact, I am using the fidget spinner for myself as an additional "reminder" since I am working on this concept and this book about Spiritual Centricity. Both its shape and the way how it is working, how it is spinning around a central axis of Centricity, remind me of the things that have become important for me and that I want to focus on even more consciously.

Therefore, I propose you to develop your own, very personal practice, your own Habit of focusing, centering your thoughts, asking yourself: what bothers me, what distracts me from what I really want to focus on now? Eliminate this source of interference and distraction as much as possible. To put it clearly: I strongly recommend that you do not eliminate the important people around you, both professionally and privately (your team, your colleagues, your family, wife/husband, or your children); on the contrary, it is

Fig. 10.2 Fidget spinner as a "reminder" for Awareness and Centricity (source: own photo)

recommended to choose these persons as your preferred Focus of Centricity. I am sure you easily understand why.

Why is this particular and conscious Focus on the important people in our close environment so important? In his book "Ich krieg dich!: Menschen für sich gewinnen," ex-secret agent Leo Martin describes his experience and practice of contacting insiders of criminal organizations and establishing relationships with these criminals (Martin 2011). As his job was to recruit liaison persons in criminal organizations such as Russian mafia organizations.

The core issue of his success was the way in which he managed to developed deep and valuable relationships. This confirms what also Bill George points out in his model of Authentic Leadership: to focus on relationships as one core success factor (George, Authentic Leadership—Rediscovering the Secrets to Creating Lasting Value, 2003). Leo Martin explains in his book in detail about his activities and experience to establish such deep and valuable relationships. His most important insights: Be attentive and show interest in the other person! Be an attentive listener, pay attention to particular topics that are of interest for the other, find things that you have in common. In other words: direct your Focus onto Awareness.

Therefore, in the end, also in relationships it is about developing Centricity of Thoughts, to consciously decide what you want to focus on and to center your Thoughts, your Awareness on it.

However, as I assume that most of you, of us do not have to deal with criminal organizations in their daily life—hopefully—I would like to lay out an example from a different area in the following section, an example that may be more familiar for many of you. It is about Focus on Awareness in photography (not only because Focus and photography are related from a technical point of view already).

Awareness in Photography

Technology has evolved a lot in photography. Such technology now becomes available for more and more people who like to do photography—not only with classical cameras but also increasingly with smartphones. A lot of Focus is today on the technical and technological side of photography: You can see and read it when you follow discussions and comments in typical online communities about photography. I am actively doing photography for more than 10 years now, and during my personal journey of continuous learning and personal development in photography, I felt increasingly uncomfortable with this strong technical and technological Focus.

Little by little, from own experience as well as from the example of other photographers that I got to know, I understood: Put aside the technology (camera) for a while and first try to understand who is the person in front of you. First try to talk to the person, or simply to exchange a smile in a true and honest way and build a bridge to that person. Then magical things can happen. This is something that I increasingly experienced myself when taking photos of persons: In photography, it is less about the technical Focus, but rather about the Focus on Awareness.

Over the years, I have come to know photographers who practice different styles of photography. From some of these photographers I learned and understood the special style of photography, which starts by approaching people in a personal, open, and respectful way. I try to live this style of photography for myself. In my own photography, I try to apply this understanding more and more, try to apply it actively. Then, magical things happen, sometimes, and over time more frequently: a shy and closed person opens up, the face starts beaming, and the eyes begin to shine.

I would like to make this more tangible with some examples from my own photography.

The First Example

I took the following portraits of a young monk during holidays in Sri Lanka while visiting a Buddhist monastery. You can see the first photo that I took in Fig. 10.3.

Like many people when you take photos of them "by surprise," he in the beginning was obviously shy and a bit embarrassed of the fact that I took a photo of him, although the photo itself is quite good from the technical point of view.

I felt his embarrassment, put down my camera, and started to talk to him. I asked his name and his age. He said "I am seventeen" and I answered "oh, then you have the same age as my son. So I could be your father and you could be my son!" Now look what happened, when I took another picture of him at that very moment, see the change in his eyes (Fig. 10.4).

Fig. 10.3 Young monk in Sri Lanka, shy (source: own photo)

The Second Example

The second example results from an evening stroll through some small downtown alleys in the southern city center of Nanjing, accompanied by a local photographer friend, visiting some non-touristic areas in the city of Nanjing, where the "real" and down-to-earth life takes place. During this walk we came across a Chinese woman who was about to prepare dinner for the family. I quickly took a few photos of her; you can see my first result in Fig. 10.5.

Just like the Buddhist monk, this Chinese woman was obviously a bit shy and somehow felt uncomfortable that we took pictures of her, even though the photos themselves have become quite nice and appealing, quite authentic. However, something was missing in the photos. The "spirit," the "essence" was missing; the inner Self of the woman was not "visible." The embarrassment and "distance" was tangible.

Fig. 10.4 Young monk in Sri Lanka—with shining eyes (source: own photo)

Fig. 10.5 Woman in Nanjing, China, shy (source: own photo)

Fig. 10.6 Woman in Nanjing, China, laughing happily (source: own photo)

However, after some nice and friendly words to the woman, including some few of myself, a little awkward because of my limited and probably funny-sounding Chinese, see for yourself what immediately happened (Fig. 10.6), look at the sincerely and happily laughing face.

The embarrassment had disappeared; the Chinese woman visibly opened up and let us see her true Self, her inner Self. There was no distance anymore, it was just human beings sharing a positive moment, spending a bit of time together, and getting to know each other as authentic people.

Therefore, what can we learn from this? If we leave the technology (camera) aside for a while and first try to really understand who that person is in front of us, just smile in a true and honest way, speak some friendly words and build a bridge to that person, then magical things can happen. This is something that I had already felt subconsciously for a long time when I took pictures of people and have now consciously understood from my years of experience. The same effect works in our Leadership situations, too, because a key aspect of Leadership is exactly to "build a bridge" to the person in front of us.

Exercise on Centricity

If you are—just like me—interested in and familiar with photography, then here is a very simple exercise that you can try:

First talk, and then shoot (a photo).

(For architecture photography, landscape photography, or other motifs, the same applies: there too it is about first "getting involved" in the motif before getting started with the camera.)
That means:

- First put aside the camera and take your time.
- To recognize how the motif for your photo "truly is".
- Try to understand and consciously see where its beauty lies.
- if it is a person, try to understand who is the person in front of you, talk to him/her,
- Simply smile in a true and honest way and build a bridge to that person.
- And only then start taking photos.
- Try using simple cameras rather than complicated DSLR cameras that too much distract your Focus onto the technology.
- And later-on, ignore comments of "tech-minded experts" judging your photos only form technical standpoint like: "ah, the focus is not correctly set onto the eye".

Then you will see things with a different view, and after some time, your photos will start to reflect that different view.

If you want to learn more about this "different" approach to photography, then I recommend you books about the psychology of photography, like Sven Barnow's book "Psychologie der Fotografie: Kopf oder Bauch?," in which he talks a lot about trustful relationships, mindfulness, and even photo-therapy in a sense of photography as path toward self-discovery and self-exploration (Barnow 2016).

Conclusion for Your Leadership

Our Thoughts have a great impact on ourselves, on our Self, but we ourselves, our Self also have an influence on our Thoughts. A chaos in our Thoughts leaves us "tumbling around;" leaving us without deeper Awareness of the current situation around us and without Awareness of the people around us, of their needs and of what concerns them.

Awareness has a huge impact on our Leadership, as the people we work with, the people around us—like everyone else around the world—are very sensitive to the presence or absence of Awareness. Working on a clear Focus on Awareness helps us to establish Centricity in our Thoughts, in ourselves.

"*Awareness*" is something that can become tangible in our impact, in our *Focus on everything around us*; when Awareness is there, it can be perceived by the people around us.

References

Barnow S (2016) Psychologie der Fotografie: Kopf oder Bauch? dpunkt, Heidelberg

George B (2003) Authentic leadership – rediscovering the secrets to creating lasting value. Wiley, San Francisco

Kingston K (2016) Clear your clutter with Feng Shui. Harmony, Crown Publishing, New York

Kingston K (2003) Feng Shui gegen das Gerümpel des Alltags. Rowohlt, Reinbek bei Hamburg

Kurth M (2018) Stell Dir vor, Du wachst auf – Die OOOO+X-Methode für mehr Präsenz und Klarheit. Rowolth, Reinbek bei Hamburg

Martin L (2011) Ich krieg dich! Menschen für sich gewinnen – Ein Ex-Agent verrät die besten Strategien. RM-Buch-und-Medien-Vertrieb, Gütersloh

Sōhō T "Taiaki – Annalen des Schwertes Taia", ca. 1600, e.g. in Takuan M (1994) ZEN in der Kunst des kampflosen Kampfes, O.W. Barth, Frankfurt a.M

Späth T, Bao SY (2011) Shaolin – Das Geheimnis der inneren Stärke. Gräfe und Unzer, München

Suzuki S (2006) Zen Mind – Beginner's Mind. Shambhala, Boston

11

Via Values to Centricity

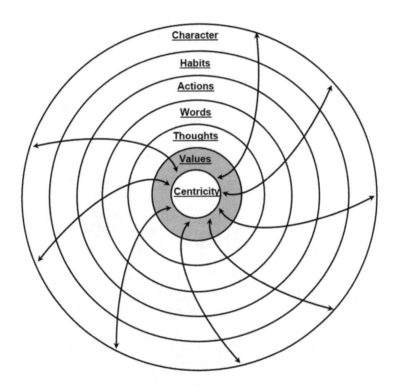

Values

The conscious, intellectual understanding of the Values—our own Values as
well as those of our respective counterpart—is an essential basis for Leadership.
As Leadership means: A Leader can never exist alone, but only in relation to

other people. A Leader is only a Leader, a "leading person" if there are people who actually follow him, who see a reason and motivation to follow. As for us as Leaders, it is our own Values that lead us, ourselves, each of us as Leaders and as human beings.

> A joy that comes from outside
>   will leave us again.
>   But those values that are rooted inside
>   are reliable and permanent.
>   (Seneca, approx. 4 B.C–65 A.C.)

What Are Values?

What do they mean for us? Again, let us first have a look at a definition of the term "Values" (Fig. 11.1):

> Value concepts, in short "values" usually describe desirable or morally well-considered properties or qualities that are assigned to objects, ideas, practical or moral ideals, facts, action patterns, character traits. [...]
>   ...

Fig. 11.1   What are Values? (source: http://www.pixabay.com, created by 905513)

The philosophy of values … [is about] … the foundation and orientation of thinking and acting according to ideational, spiritual values. [...]

…

Ideational values are understood as [...] an inner enrichment, a maturation of the personality…. (translated from Wikipedia 2018a)

From this definition, it gets clear why Values lie at a deeper level in the concept of Spiritual Leadership, which forms a basis for Character, Habits, Actions, Words, and Thoughts, a basis which influences them and which gives direction for these higher levels. It means that you can work on a very "deep," inner and therefore essential level if you focus on your Values and work consciously and carefully with them, in full Awareness of these Values and of what they mean to you.

This chapter is about getting to know your Values, because our Values are a core driver of what we appreciate, what we like, what we do not like, and even what makes us angry. Values not only determine our behavior, they also influence our decisions and influence our judgements. Being aware of our Values and consciously focusing on our Values, we gain more stability, security, and continuity in our actions, because this understanding, this Awareness, and this Focus help us to express what we really stand for. They give us a natural, authentic Centricity of our personality and our Character. The people around us will be able to feel the natural authenticity that this Centricity gives us.

Maybe you have already heard of concepts like Value-Based Leadership. In that respect, I would like to refer again to Bill George, who in his book "Authentic Leadership—Rediscovering the Secrets to Creating Lasting Value" puts great emphasis on Values as drivers of our behavior (George 2003).

On the one hand, Bill George creates a balance between Values and performance in his book, with the clear message that Values and performance are not mutually exclusive, but rather that stable Values and a Value-oriented culture are the basis for lasting performance and success, personally for a Leader, as well as for companies and organizations. He states that Values are not simply "there," but must be actively communicated, lived, and exemplified, they must flow into Words and Actions, become Habits and manifest in our Thoughts, in our culture. Bill George already implicitly addresses an understanding as laid out in the dynamic level concept of Spiritual Leadership and Centricity presented here.

Another interesting thing that Bill George describes is how every new employee at his company Medtronic receives a "medallion" that is meant to be a symbol of his personal affiliation with the Medtronic company. You may remember that, in previous chapters, we heard about the symbolism of a Totem or a "reminder," which can help you to focus on important elements of Centricity. The medallion at Medtronic is also a kind of Totem, which represents the Character of the company and which allows the employee to participate in the Character of the company and reminds him constantly of it.

Now, how do you get to know your own Values? It is usually not enough to just quickly think about our Values and write them down. Here I would like to show you a way how you can develop a better understanding of your core Values based on psychological findings concerning role behavior and Values. In our company within the Bosch Group, methods for determining a person's Values are used in Leadership trainings, supported by the consulting company Axialent (see Axialent website 2018).

Determining Your Values

In Chap. 7 we have already focused on the importance of Roles and our own understanding of Roles in Leadership. It is now important to understand how the Roles that we live—and the respective Role behavior that we live—arise and what influences them. As already mentioned, we can actively develop our own, personal picture of our Role as a Leader, and thereby influence how we live our Role as a Leader.

However, as explained in the previous section, there are factors that fundamentally—and very permanently—influence our behavior patterns, our Role behavior, namely our Values. Our Values are particularly formed by persons from our close environment, by persons that we use for orientation—consciously or unconsciously—and who thereby shape our own Role behavior. To be more precisely: by persons who have been—or are still—shaping the basis of our Role behavior, namely our Values.

In literature, these interdependencies have already been clearly worked out, so the groundwork for determining our Values is already known from there. For example, in Wikipedia we can find the following under the keyword "role model":

Sociologists and psychologists [deal] with [...] role models in the immediate social environment (parents, peer group), whose behavior is mimicked unconsciously [...]. (translated from Wikipedia 2018b)

In the Wikipedia encyclopedia, we find this summarized in the definition of the term "role model":

A role model is a person or thing that is regarded as a trend-setting and idealized pattern or example. In the narrower sense, a role model is a person with whom a—usually young—person identifies and whose behavior patterns he imitates or tries to imitate. (translated from Wikipedia 2018b)

Now we know that there are not only—as described above—positive Role models in our social environment who give us orientation, and who lead to positive influences. There are also negative Role models, also called "bad examples," who can leave a negative or "inverse imprint" or coinage on us, in a sense that we object to their bad example, because their characteristics are in contradiction to what we stand for. We will get to that in a moment.

However, what exactly is it that these Role models from our family and peer group imprint on us, what is their effect on us, our ourselves, our Self? To answer this question we for example find the explanation in the "Enzyklopädie der Wertvorstellungen" (Encyclopedia of Values, www.wertsysteme.de) that Role models shape, influence, and "imprint" our Values (Website Enzyklopädie der Wertesysteme 2018). This means that by their behavior and Actions, by what Role models exemplify us, and because we perceive their behavior and Actions as an example, our own Value system arises, is shaped, and imprinted on us. The meaning of the word "imprint" or "coinage" as the origin meaning of the term "Character" was already discussed in Chap. 6.

Role models thus shape our Values, and it is our Values that underlie our own Role behavior, on an inner level of Centricity.

With all these insights, you have a valuable source at hand for determining your own Values, because: By focusing on the characteristics of people from your social environment who left an "imprint" on you, and by translating their characteristics into Values, you can discover the source of your own personal Values, the core Values of yourself, your Self. We will now do a little exercise on this.

Exercise on Centricity

Draw two "Value circles" as shown in Fig. 11.2 below. Then, ask yourself the following questions:

1. First in the positive sense:

   - Which people from your family or peer environment (managers, colleagues, employees, and friends) used to be or are Role models for you today?
   - And how have these people shaped you positively, what do these people stand for?
   - In the sectors of the first Value circle, write down the most important *positive* "imprints" or coinage that you have experienced from those people who were or are a role model for you.

2. Now the other way round:

   - Which people were negative Role models for you, so to say: "bad examples"?
   - What "imprints" or coinage did these people leave on you, based on what these people stand for?
   - In the sectors of the second Value circle, first write down the most important *negative* characteristics that you have experienced in these people.
   - Now invert these negative characteristics, write down the corresponding complementary *inverted* imprints for each negative characteristic (such as unfair ↔ fair, stingy ↔ generous, lazy ↔ hardworking).

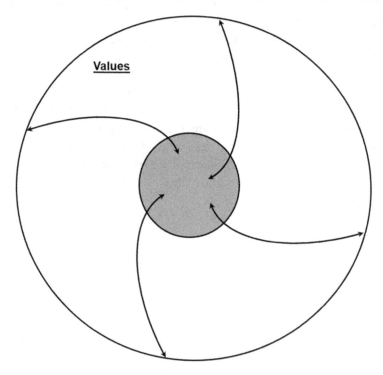

Fig. 11.2 Value Circle

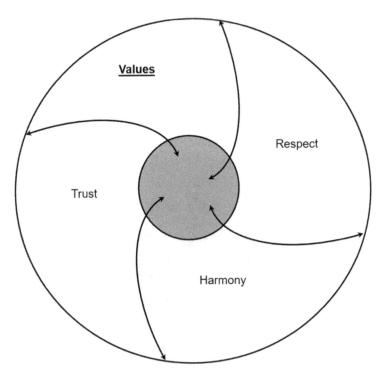

Fig. 11.3 Values—derived from positive Role models and "imprints" (source: own drawing)

Coming from the positive Role model and positive imprint, the result can for example look as shown in Fig. 11.3. Alternatively—coming from the negative Role model and inverted imprint—the result can look as shown in Fig. 11.4.

I propose you to do this exercise for several positive and negative Role models and their respective imprints. Then look which characteristics, which Values accumulate in the sectors of the value circle, which occur repeatedly.

These "imprints" that you have found and written down, especially those that accumulate in the Value circle, that occur repeatedly, are most likely strong Values which are "imprinted" as a coinage in yourself, they are your core Values! Because it is the coinage caused by the behavior of Role models in the family and peer group—such behavior being based on their own Values—which most likely has shaped these core Values in yourself, in your Self. Alternatively, it is at least that, in the current behavior of Role models, you now recognize your own, already shaped Values, such that the Role model behavior resonates with your own Values, in a positive or negative sense.

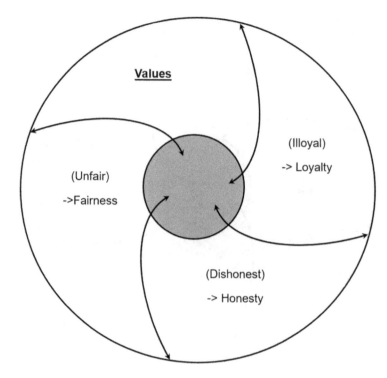

Fig. 11.4 Values—derived from negative Role models and converted to "inverted imprints" (source: own drawing)

Using Your Values Consciously

When you have identified your core Values that are at the Center of your personality, then actively focus on them and build a conscious Centricity of your Self based on these Values, with a conscious Focus on the outer levels of Centricity that lie above the level of Values. Use the understanding of your Values for strengthening our Leadership, in the sense and understanding of Spiritual Leadership.

Character

As pointed out in Chap. 6, your Character is something very stable, long lasting. As a result, your Character "characterizes" you as a person, or better: as a personality, because your Character is a kind of "overall summary" of your personality. The knowledge of your own Values, your core Values, will not change your Character. The knowledge of your Values, your core Values will not change anything about how you really *are*.

But this knowledge can help you to make yourself more aware of your own, true Character and, on this basis, help you to make more *visible and tangible* for others around you who and how you really are. Because your Character is the outer appearance of your personality that is tangible for others.

This experience and tangibility of your true and thus naturally authentic personality materializes on the subsequent levels of the concept of Centricity, of Spiritual Leadership.

Habits

In Chap. 7, I recommended you to define an analogy, a picture for your own Leadership. Based on the knowledge of your Values, your core Values, you can compare whether the picture you have chosen actually corresponds to yourself, your Self, namely to your Values, i.e., to what you as a person, as a personality actually stand for.

Reflect your personal picture of your own Leadership Role on the (core) Values you have found for yourself. Does the picture of your Leadership Role match these Values; can they be found in this picture, in this analogy? If not, then work again on your picture of your Leadership Role, question it and, if necessary, define an adapted picture that fits better to your core Values, that reflects them better.

Actions

As explained in Chap. 8, Actions are something that we can do consciously and purposefully and that we can control, according to our motives. Via this, we can step in very consciously and cross-check and align our Actions with our Values, our core Values. As Viktor Frankl (1905–1997), Austrian neurologist and psychiatrist said:

> You cannot teach values
>   You can only live them.

Based on the understanding and knowledge of our Values, especially of our core Values, we can always compare our behavior, our Actions with our core Values in order to verify whether we ourselves, whether our Self and our Actions are in line with these Values. Because if this is not the case, then our behavior, our Actions are not "centered," then we move outside of our Center, outside of our Focus. Then we start to "tumble" and lose valuable energy.

So if—in a certain moment—you ask yourself the question: "What should I do now?," then remember your core Values, work out for yourself the different options for Actions, and reflect them on your core Values. Then focus on the option that reflects the core, the Center of your Values. Because this is the option that arises from yourself, from the Center of your Self. Such Value-focused and Value-centered Action will strengthen your Leadership, out of your personal Centricity.

Words

In Chap. 9, we have already learned how powerful Words can be, how much power and influence even some few Words can have if they are well chosen. It is very important for us as Leaders *what* we say and *how* we say it.

A basis and an orientation for the choice of your Words—and for how to use them in order to strengthen your Leadership—are your Values, your core Values. Although Viktor Frankl rightly said, "You cannot teach values, you can only live them," Words can nevertheless support our Actions and their effects, their impact. Our Words can help to focus other people's perception of our Actions on what we want to convey, on what is important for us, on what we stand for.

Exercise on Centricity

If, for example, you as a Leader explain a decision for a certain course of Action to other people, you can proceed as follows and use the following Words:

- First make your guiding Values, transparent for the people around you, in strong, clear Words: "For me, fairness is very important, therefore...."
- Then consciously crosscheck the options for Action against your Values: "Would it be fair if...?"
- Finally, formulate your evaluation, your assessment and your decision for Action clearly and in accordance with your Values: "From a fairness perspective, I decided for the following option..."

I now use this type of communication myself often consciously, both concerning the choice of my Words as well as the way I use Words. For me personally—at least in my personal, subjective perception—this has significantly changed something for myself, both in my decision-making and my Actions as well as in my personal commitment to and my communication of such decisions and Actions. I am convinced that this will—gradually and increasingly—have an impact on the persons around me.

Thoughts

As already explained in the previous Chap. 10, the understanding of our counterpart—i.e., the competence of "Awareness"—has a big influence on our Leadership. This Awareness ultimately takes place in our mind, in our Thoughts. You will surely remember the quote from Sun Tsu "The Art of War" (Sūnzi Bīngfǎ 孙子兵法; Sun Tsu 2007) which reads:

> Zhī jǐ (Know yourself)
> zhī bǐ   (and know your counterpart,)
> bǎi zhàn   (then a hundred conflicts)
> bǎi sheng   (will turn into a hundred successes.)
> (Tsu, 500 B.C) chapter

This quote, especially the part "Know your counterpart" ultimately expresses the importance of Awareness in our Thoughts for our success when dealing with our respective counterpart.

The people we work with, the people around us—like all people worldwide—are very sensitive to the presence or lack of Awareness. As already mentioned, "Awareness" is something that can becomes tangible in our impact, in our Focus on everything around us. When Awareness is there, it that can be perceived by the people around us.

It is important to note that "Awareness" is already a Value in itself. So if you recognize that Awareness is a core Value for yourself, then use it consciously and actively, because it can become a strong basis for successful Leadership. Awareness also means to recognize via our conscious outward Focus, via the conscious Focus on our counterpart, to attentively recognize his respective Values and to consciously perceive them. Because these Values of our counterpart are the building blocks of *his* Character, *his* Habits and Actions, *his* Words and Thoughts.

Conclusion for Your Leadership

By understanding the Character and importance of Values in every human being, in ourselves and in our respective counterpart, we as Leaders can create a strong basis for our own Leadership, as well as for the relationships with our respective counterparts. If we develop an Awareness, a Centricity for those (core) Values, these Values can be experienced and become tangible for ourselves as well as for our respective counterpart on the different levels of Spiritual Leadership:

> In our Character
>> In our Habits
>> In our behavior, our Actions
>> In our Words
>> In our Thoughts, in particular in our Awareness

The intellectual, spiritual understanding of the Values—our own Values as well as those of our respective counterpart—is an essential basis for Leadership. That is what Leadership means: A Leader is only a Leader, i.e., a leading person, if there are people who actually follow him. A Leader can never exist alone, but only in relation to other people. As for us as Leaders, it is our own Values that guide us as Leaders, each of us.

References

Axialent-Website (2018) https://www.axialent.com/

George B (2003) Authentic leadership – rediscovering the secrets to creating lasting value. Wiley, San Francisco

Sun Tsu " The Art of War" (Sūnzi Bīngfǎ 孙子兵法), about 500 B.C., e.g.in: Luo Zhiye (translator) (2007) Sun Tzu's The Art of War, Chinese Classical Treasury (Chinese-English Edition), Zhongguo Chuban Jituan, Beijing, ISBN 978-7-5001-1812-1

Wikipedia (2018a) Wertvorstellung. Wikipedia Die freie Enzyklopädie. https://de. wikipedia.org/wiki/Wertvorstellung. Accessed May 22, 2018

Wikipedia (2018b) Vorbild. Wikipedia Die freie Enzyklopädie. https://de.wikipedia. org/wiki/Vorbild. Accessed May 22, 2018

Website Enzyklopädie der Wertesysteme (2018) https://www.wertesysteme.de/ was-sind-werte/

12

Getting to the Core: Mindfulness and Inner Centricity

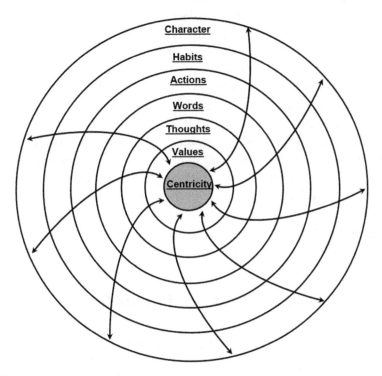

Centricity (source: own drawing)

When we turn our Focus towards the inside,
  when we calm our mind and decelerate,
  when we discover our inner center, our inner Centricity,
  then we can free our Self from burdening clutter

T. H. Ulrich, *Spiritual Leadership*, https://doi.org/10.1007/978-3-030-45432-6_12

and achieve a spiritual state that we call "Mindfulness."
(Thomas Ulrich 2018)

In the previous chapters, I wrote quite a lot about working on and development of Centricity at different levels of the concept of Spiritual Leadership. For some of you it may still be difficult to "grasp" what Centricity really means and how to deal with it. In particular, you may still find it difficult to separate the Thoughts at just at this very moment are valuable and helpful for this moment from such ones that hinder you at this moment, which are "clutter" in your mind, which cause confusion and which make you "tumble." The intention of this chapter is to give you instructions on how to work on and how to develop your inner Centricity, from which Centricity and impact on the higher levels of Spiritual Leadership arise in a very natural way.

Why should we—as Leaders—consider working on inner Centricity? One reason: Because we are all living in a much more dynamic environment today, working on multiple tasks at the same time and are often so busy with all kinds of things that we forget to take a moment to just lean back, close our eyes, and just breathe. To draw energy from ourselves, from our Self, from within, an energy that truly helps us to develop a strong, authentic, and even Spiritual Leadership.

We should not forget another aspect, which becomes obvious from the analogy of the gyro at the beginning of the book: If the masses move outside their center and "tumble around," then the gyro loses energy and becomes increasingly unstable. He can keep on tumbling for some time, but "it burns more and more energy," and eventually, topples down. Inner Centricity helps us to avoid "to become burnt out," which we all know as "burn out syndrome" in professional life today.

The Core of Mindfulness and Inner Centricity

Now we really get to the core, to the truly essential core of Centricity. Because I am fully convinced: without working on the inner Centricity, all of our activities on the other levels risk to become superficial or even ridiculous. However, if we develop a strong and stable inner Centricity, like a gyro, with its axis centered and fully aligned along the gravitational field, then everything else will naturally fall into place, like the masses that move around the stable inner axis of the gyro.

A character, a mind, and a soul with a calm and stable inner Centricity will naturally develop an overlying level of positive and strong core Values such as respect, fairness, honesty, and reliability. The inner energy source that drives these core Values, the inner Centricity, remains unchanged and stable, like the trunk of a tree, and forms the "center of gravity" of your Character, your mind, and your soul.

The same also applies for the other, subsequent outer levels of Spiritual Leadership, as from the calm and stable inner Centricity you will develop clarity and Awareness in your Thoughts, as well as the ability to consciously focus your mind on the essential things. Your Words will naturally become respectful and strong and will derive their strength from the stability and energy of inner Centricity. Your Actions will reflect your inner Centricity. In your Habits you will become clear and stable in your own Role and you can become a Role model for others. Your Character will naturally become even more concise and tangible for the people around you.

> This inward spiritual Focus is what we call "Mindfulness."
> Moreover, this Mindfulness is the basis for inner Centricity.

However, how do you develop this Mindfulness, this inner Centricity? Let us delve deeper into philosophy, especially Asian philosophy, to answer this question. First, I would like to recall the Chinese proverb from the beginning of this book:

Huó dào lǎo, xué dào lǎo
    Live until old, learn until old.

Therefore, be aware: Working on inner Centricity is actually a lifelong path, a lifelong journey. However, for characters, for personalities who enjoy working continuously on developing their own personality and who see every step of their development as a step of joy and success, this path can be a source of constant encouragement, energy, and satisfaction. As another saying goes: "The way is the goal" (often attributed to Confucius).

Let Us Start with the Basics: The Posture

As Miyamoto Musashi wrote in his "Book of the Five Rings":

When your body is relaxed,
    do not let your spirit slacken.

But when your body
is in violent motion,
stay calm in your spirit.
Never let your spirit
be torn away
by the action
of the body,
and never let your body
be influenced by your spirit. (translated from Musashi, 1645)

Inner centricity in posture (Fig. 12.1) begins with little things. Simple things. We just have to remember them and consciously work on them.

The first thing to do is to develop a centered and upright posture and to maintain this while sitting, standing, or walking. We find such practice being taught and practiced especially in Asian (martial) arts; see for example the already mentioned book of Linda Myoki Lehrhaupt "T'ai Chi as a Path to Wisdom" (Lehrhaupt 2013). I have learned such practice myself in the Japanese sword art Iaido, and it can also be found in meditation practices, as

Fig. 12.1 The posture (Source: http://www.pixabay.com, created by kalhh, amended)

described, for example, by Christopher Klein and Jens Helbig (2017) and Thomas Gamsjäger (2016). I will discuss their books in more detail later. In his book "LEADING from WITHIN" (Prater 1988), Robert Prater also stresses the importance of posture and its effect on our physical and mental power.

Let us understand what a centered and upright posture means.

Imagine that a thread is attached to your skullcap, which pulls the skullcap upward and thereby stretches your spine upward, into an upright position (see Fig. 12.2). Feel actively how your skullcap moves upward. You will feel the inner Centricity that your body develops by actively and consciously focusing on this posture (I assume that women should be more familiar with this kind of posture, because—according to my limited understanding as a

Fig. 12.2 Posture and Centricity (source: http://www.pixabay.com, created by GDJ, amended)

Fig. 12.3 Meditation stool (source: own photo)

man—this also happens when wearing shoes with high heels). Work on this posture when standing and when sitting. You will experience how you gain more presence and visibility for yourself and for others.

A good way to get a feeling for this posture is to sit on a meditation cushion or meditation stool (Fig. 12.3). I myself like to use a meditation stool, which you can see in the following figure, because it relieves the legs, the weight rests on the stool. Otherwise, one would sit directly on the heels with undercut legs. Thus, using such stool, there is no risk—especially for us "Westerners"—that in the unusual position, the legs fall asleep or hurt and our focus would be distracted.

This type of meditation cushion or meditation stool supports the spine, brings it into an upright position, and you may even find that you can sit more comfortably, more relaxed, and above all more centered on such a cushion or stool than on your office chair, on which one quickly tends to "loll about" or slump down. It is not without reason that in the army a soldier is taught to adopt an upright posture when commanded to "snap to attention," because the outer posture also affects the inner posture.

I recommend to consciously using the strength and inner Centricity of this posture and its effect on others, especially in situations where you want to make a strong impact, which is true—in the extreme—even in conflict situations. This centered and at the same time relaxed posture will send a message to your counterpart (your conflict opponent) that you feel completely self-confident, and this can make your counterpart refrain from conflicting with you.

Does that sound unrealistic to you? Well, there is a story about a Buddhist monk who was forced into a sword duel by a samurai (see for example in Paul

J. Kohtes' book "Dein Job ist es, frei zu sein—Zen und die Kunst des Managements"). The poor monk had absolutely no idea about sword fencing. On the other hand, he had no chance to avoid the duel in that situation. So what should he do? The only thing he could do was to do what he was best in: He took a posture of complete self-centeredness, of a centered Self, centered in himself, calmly raising the sword high above his head. It is said that the samurai was so impressed and unsettled by this calm and Self-Centricity that he quit the duel and threw away his sword.

The Body Energy

Not only when sitting, standing, or walking will you experience a change when you focus on your center, when you focus on inner Centricity. We have already heard about the energy center in Chap. 8 (Japanese Hara—腹 or Chinese "lower Dantian" 下丹田—Xià Dāntián), which is about three finger widths below the navel and two finger widths inside the body, and in Asia is considered as the "source of life and energy" in our body. Historically, the first detailed description of the lower Dantian can be found in the Daoist writings of Lao Tse, which date back to the sixth century BC (Lǎozǐ zhōng jīng 老子中經). This Hara or lower Dantian is the point of maximum physical inner Centricity in our body. According to Asian philosophy, the energy for body, mind, and soul originates from the Hara or lower Dantian. As already mentioned, a detailed description can be found in Karlfried Graf Dürckheim's book "Hara" (Dürckheim 2012).

I know this may sound strange and rather esoteric to western people. However, I have made the experience that many things you do with our body become much more energetic and powerful when you start from your Hara. You can experience and feel it in particular in body movements that require a lot of strength and energy. By consciously focusing on this source of life and energy, you will be able to make your movements more powerful, but you can also experience something happening inside you "within yourself." Therefore, the teachers or masters of Asian martial arts teach their students that these punching, kicking, and blocking techniques must be performed starting from the Hara.

A quite famous example and proof for the power of body movements performed from the Hara is the so-called "One Inch Punch" developed by Bruce Lee. You can find videos about this "One Inch Punch" on the Internet. When you watch closely, especially in slow motion videos of it, you will see that Bruce Lee performs the punch starting from the Hara, not just from the hand or arm. He draws the power of the punch from the Hara as the "source of life and energy" in his body.

As already mentioned in Chap. 8, the lower Dantian or Hara is closely related to breathing when it is done as "right breathing," as centered breathing from the abdomen. Many books and literature deal in detail with "right breathing" from the lower Dantian or Hara, a centered breathing that originates from the energy center of the human being, and with the conscious Focus on this centered breathing as a further step toward inner Centricity. In the next section, I will go into more detail on literature on this topic.

Exercise on Centricity

In order to get a first feeling for the meaning of the "right, centered breathing" out of the lower Dantian or Hara, I recommend you an exercise, based on the principle of Pranayama meditation. This meditation is explained for example by Christopher Klein and Jens Helbig in their little booklet "Meditation für Anfänger" (Klein and Helbig 2017) or by Thomas Gamsjäger in his also very compact booklet with the same title "Meditation für Anfänger" (Gamsjäger 2016). We will later hear about some English language literature for meditation. Here the exercise:

- Sit in an upright posture with your legs undercut, as described in the previous section (as said I highly recommend using a meditation cushion or stool).
- Close your eyes halfway, so that you see your surroundings as if through a light veil.
- Consciously use abdominal breathing: Breathe slowly and deeply into your abdomen, feel how your abdomen expands with every breath, and how your abdomen slowly contracts when you exhale, to slowly push out the air again.
- Focus on your breath.
- Feel your breath slowly and deeply entering through your nose, filling your lungs down to your diaphragm, to your abdomen, and then slowly exiting the same path upward again.
- Consciously pay attention to how the breath moves with each inhalation to the spot below your navel, to the Hara.

Maybe you already feel a kind of "warmth" or "energy" being created at the location of the Hara, and that gradually penetrates and fills your whole body.

So now, we have together developed a first feeling for the lower Dantian or Hara. Fine. Nevertheless, you might ask yourself, and rightly so: why should you, should we as Leaders care for this Hara/Dantian?

I am sure you can already guess the reason:

A classical way—especially in Asian cultures—to achieve inner Centricity is through meditative techniques and meditative practice. These techniques and practices often start by working on one's own posture, breathing, and feeling for the body's energy centers. These are the entrance to the path to consciously and sustainably center your thoughts, consciousness, and mind, and thus to achieve Mindfulness and finally inner Centricity.

So let us take a closer look at meditative techniques and meditative practice and let us get a better understanding of them.

About Meditative Techniques and Meditative Practice

One thing to make clear in advance:

In this book, I do not intend to present detailed instructions on *HOW* to practice meditation and meditation techniques—because there are already a lot of and very detailed publications about meditation, some of which I will deal with as examples. My intention is rather to explain *WHY* it can be meaningful for Leaders to practice meditation, be it in its true sense, or in general as meditative techniques and meditative exercises (Fig. 12.4, with kind permission of Da Bao'en Temple "Temple of Thanksgiving" 报恩寺—Bào ēn Sì in Nanjing).

Thus:

What is the "added value" or the "return on investment" of meditation, meditative techniques, meditative practice and exercises for a Leader and manager? There are two main things:

1. Clarity of mind and thoughts:
   Essential basis for Leadership and management, especially with regard to strategic planning, evaluations, and decision-making.
2. Recognizing and leaving your own "comfort zone":
   Essential basis for any substantial and sustainable personal self-development.

As Rev. Mel Zabel correctly wrote in his book "Meditation… It's not what you think" (Zabel 2013), meditation is ultimately a training of the spirit, a "mind training," i.e., a training of Mindfulness. In western culture, this is often seen equal to contemplation. For me, contemplation is just one possible

Fig. 12.4 Meditation (source: own photo)

form of meditation and training of Mindfulness or mind training, but it is by far not the only way and form of meditative practice.

Meditation and meditative techniques help us and lead us to freeing our own mind. To free the mind from clinging to "useless" thoughts, i.e., from mental "clutter," and to avoid getting tangled and lost in a chaos of thoughts. Through clarity and Focus of the mind, through Mindfulness, one can achieve an inner Centricity, which also materializes as Focus and Centricity on the outer levels of the Spiritual Leadership concept, and which can be perceived by others as Focus and Centricity of Values, Thoughts, Words, Actions, etc.

There are many different types of meditation or meditative techniques and exercises, known from different—mostly Asian—cultures. Of course, we know

about forms of meditation "as such," where a contemplative or spiritual meditation is at the center of the practice, such as:
Buddhist meditation practice, for example

- Zen meditation
- Vipassana meditation (stemming from Theravada Buddhism, comprising a technique to focus on one's own breath)

Chinese forms of meditation, for example:

- Taoist meditation (practiced in different forms, e.g., as meditation of breath, emptiness, or visualization)

or Hindu forms of meditation, for example:

- Mantra meditation (the best known of which is probably the meditation practice that uses the syllable "Om" as a mantra)
- Yogic meditation forms (such as Kundalini meditation or the already mentioned Pranayama meditation)

On the other hand, there are also meditative arts and practices in which the meditative character is kind of an "add-on" that plays a more or less important role in the art, where the art practice is—at a first glance—the primary Focus and at the center of the respective practice. Some of such arts are:
Physical exercises with meditative character, for example:

- Indian yoga
- The Chinese Qi Gong

or martial arts with meditative spirit, for example:

- The already mentioned Japanese archery Kyūdō
- The Japanese sword art Iaidō
- The Chinese Tai Chi, also described in previous chapters

Moreover, let us not forget about Christian contemplative practice (or comparable practice in other religions and cultures): religious Mindfulness through prayer, religious contemplation or mystical spirituality. Ruben Habito lays out in his book "Living Zen, Loving God" (Habito 1995, German publication "Zen leben—Christ bleiben", Habito 2006) that meditation, spirituality, and Christian religion are by no means controversial, but can rather be complementary. I would like to take a closer look at this form of religious Mindfulness in following sections.

Last but not least, even everyday activities and actions can have meditative character or can be carried out in a meditative way. For example, you may have heard of Buddhist monks who practice gardening as a form of meditation, such as raking Zen gardens (Japanese: Kare-san-sui 枯 山水, meaning "dry landscape"). For myself, I recognized that I really like to iron my shirts myself. I was surprised to discover that and wondered why. It struck me that ironing shirts has a calming and almost contemplative effect on me: the simplicity of the movements, the Focus on the purely mechanical execution of the movements, letting the mind come to rest, and focusing the mind to the task of avoiding wrinkles in the fabric. All of this is actually a form of Mindfulness, a very practical way of meditation technique.

Meditative Techniques and Meditative Practice in Literature and in Personal Life

If you would like to become more familiar with the meditation practice (Fig. 12.5) via publications in literature in order to find your own way of meditation for yourself, I recommend you to start with books that give a first overview of different meditation techniques. You may start with David Fontana: "The Meditation Handbook: The Practical Guide to Eastern and Western Meditation Techniques," (Fontana 1999) or Geshe Kelsang Gyatso: "The New Meditation Handbook" (Gyatso 2013).

Another example is Emma Mills' book "Inhale—Exhale—Repeat: A meditation handbook for every part of your day" (Mills 2017). The title is a bit misleading, because Mills describes very practical methods for turning a daily routine into a series of exercises on Awareness and Mindfulness. From my personal point of view, these methods are suitable for people who prefer to do rather small steps of Awareness and Mindfulness practice "en passant" in their everyday life.

Of course, your personal expectations and your personal preferences will lead you to decide which book and what type of meditative practice you may find most appealing for yourself. Personally, I consider small beginner's books like the booklet "Meditation für Anfänger" by Christopher Klein and Jens Helbig (2017) a very good start, especially for (busy) Leaders and managers. Such kind of booklets are very compact, clear, and concise, so to speak one "Executive Summary" on the meaning and practice of meditation, especially

Fig. 12.5 Meditative practice (source: http://www.pixabay.com, created by Ben_ Kerckx, amended)

from a western culture perspective. Another beginner's booklet with the same title "Meditation für Anfänger" by Thomas Gamsjäger (2016) goes in a similar direction. In it, the author describes many practical exercises and meditation techniques that can be carried out in a relatively short exercise time of 10–30 min. Gamsjäger even describes a mini-meditation that only lasts a minute or even just a moment.

The main message of such books is:

Better a bit of meditation than no meditation at all

After all, the proverb is true that goes "constant dripping wears the stone." Constantly working on Mindfulness, making this practice an integral part of your way of life, a target or path that you always return to, be it even if just for a moment, will finally have a lasting effect.

I personally value literature very much that deals with practical meditation experiences of western practitioners, such as Rev. Mel Zabel: "Meditation… It's not what you think" (Zabel 2013). In this book, he describes in detail and very insistently, that meditation is a very personal thing and not a pre-made scheme or "cooking recipe" of any guru. He makes very clear what effect personal meditative practice can have on the direct environment, the people around you, if one finally achieves Mindfulness and inner Centricity through meditation and meditative practices.

Indeed that is what characterizes, what makes a good Leader:

- Having an impact on our environment, on the people around us
- To put our personal "imprint" onto our environment
- And to develop and establish Habits
- In line with our Thoughts
- And based on our Values
- To convey them with strong, clear Words
- That express what our Character stands for
- And to turn them consequently into Actions
- Thereby inspiring and leading others to such way of consequent and consistent acting

My personal experience is that, for a western mind and spirit, as well as in a western culture and environment, many things are based on Actions rather than purely contemplative practice. A meditative practice that involves some kind of Actions therefore generally fits better to our cultural environment than a purely contemplative path such as Zen meditation, especially when such Zen path is mainly focussing on Zazen practice, a practice of sitting while concentrating on breath, thought, and silent meditation for quite a long time. See, for example, the book of Shunryu Suzuki "Zen Mind—Beginner's Mind" (Suzuki 2006, German publication: Suzuki 1975), and some more books for readers with German language skills: Eugen Herriegel "Der Zen-Weg" (Herriegel 1958) or Irmgard Schloegel "Was ist Zen" (Schloegel 1995).

The western Focus on Actions is probably an explanation why yoga practice is much more successful in the west than Zen practice. Western approaches to meditative techniques and Mindfulness tend to focus on activities rather than pure contemplation, such as the "tools and recipes" that Emma Mills wrote in her already mentioned book "Inhale—Exhale—Repeat: A meditation handbook for every part of your day" (Mills 2017).

As mentioned earlier, there are practices or "arts" that involve Actions or activity but still have a strong Focus on meditative practice and spirituality and—if taught and practiced properly—also include a strong part of breathing practice, Awareness, Mindfulness, and Centricity of mind, all of it combined in a holistic practice. However, from my personal experience, such a holistic practice and accordingly oriented teachers are not easy to find in the western world.

In this book, we have already heard of meditative arts, such as yoga, Japanese archery Kyūdō, Japanese sword art Iaidō, Chinese Tai Chi, or Chinese Qi Gong, and of reference to various books and writings, such as those by Hellriegel, Chozuan, and Sōhō. Some of these meditative—and therefore spiritual—arts can be practiced with relatively little logistic efforts, and can be practiced at any time and almost anywhere, such as Tai Chi, Yoga, or Qi Gong. Others need more space and specific equipment, and experienced spiritual teachers are more difficult to find, such as for the practice of Japanese archery Kyūdō and Japanese sword art Iaidō.

We had already heard Shissai Chozuan from "Tengu-Geijutsu-Ron—Discourse on the Art of the Mountain Demons" (on the true principle of sword art) in a previous chapter:

> There are many arts, and if you wanted to practice each one, one life would not be enough to master them. If, however, you let your heart completely melt in one single art, then you will also know about the other arts, even without having any practical experience in them. (translated from: Chozuan 1728)

It is therefore sufficient to find for yourself one specific, suitable art, to find a suitable practice that fits you, and to consciously and continuously focus on it. It is important to choose it according to your own preconditions. As an example, I would like to give you a suggestion that goes into a slightly different direction than the meditation practices and meditative arts already mentioned:

Since managers and Leaders generally have little spare time and are always busy with many other things (at least that is what many managers say), I would like to introduce you to a spiritual and meditative art that is easy to practice, anytime, anywhere, even in the office, on the plane or in the hotel room: the art of calligraphy.

For myself, I discovered by chance and rather incidentally (while I was learning Chinese and practicing Chinese characters) the calming and contemplative effect of calligraphy, performing the movements of the hand holding the pen and designing the lines of Chinese characters in a concentrated and focused way (Fig. 12.6), thereby discovering an increasing experience of inner peace.

Fig. 12.6 Calligraphy of Chinese characters (source: own photo)

This experience was confirmed by the book by H.E. Davey "Brush Meditation" (Davey 1999), which I found in a literature search after my personal discovery of the effect of calligraphy. Davey describes the harmony of body and mind, which can be achieved through Shodō—the Japanese way (Dō) of calligraphy. Davey points out that Japanese calligraphy in Japan is considered "an image of the mind" and this is expressed in a Japanese proverb as follows:

Kokoro tadashikereba sunawachi fude tadashii.

which can be translated as:

If your mind is correct, then the brush is correct.

Therefore, it is mainly about the mind, about the "attitude of the mind" or "mindset," and the brush, the "attitude of the brush" is (only) a tool to consciously and sustainably focus your own thoughts, consciousness, and your mind, i.e., your mindfulness. This practice does not require a lot of material, it does not require many material things:

You do not even need a sophisticated calligraphy equipment with brushes, ink, etc. All you need is a special calligraphy pen, be it a calligraphy fountain pen or a special calligraphy brush pen, which I prefer for Chinese calligraphy. The tip of such a calligraphy pen is specially designed to draw beautiful lines, letters, or characters, as it enables the calligrapher to shape the lines of letters or characters, to give them an individual style and character, or more precise: make them a visible expression of your Character.

Here, too, everything starts with the posture: as already described previously, here too the first step is to adopt and maintain a centered and upright posture, as if a thread were attached to your skullcap that pulls the skullcap up and thereby stretches your spine into an upright posture. To achieve such a posture, I again recommend using a meditation cushion or meditation stool and a low table to write, to draw your calligraphy on. Of course, you can also write on a normal chair and at an ordinary table if you consciously maintain an upright, centered posture. On such "normal" furniture, it is just more difficult to maintain a centered and upright posture. Once in this posture, move the pen or brush slowly and carefully while observing your breath, consciously feel the breath, and center your mind, the same was as for a practice of contemplative meditation as already described.

Practicing this way, with full Mindfulness and focused on consciously designing line by line at a time, you may experience a calming of your breathing and thoughts at the same time, while gaining increasing Mindfulness and inner Centricity of the mind. Until, finally, it is no longer yourself who is consciously writing, drawing the lines of the calligraphy, but "It" is writing. Exactly as Eugen Herriegel describes in his already cited book Zen in the Art of Archery as the "goal" of Kyūdō: that finally, the archer no longer is the one shooting, but that "It" is shooting (Herriegel 1989, German publication "Zen in der Kunst des Bogenschießens," Herriegel 1999).

If you decide to try the art of calligraphy by yourself, I recommend you to practice the art of calligraphy not just with any arbitrary characters, words, or sentences, but rather with characters, words, or sentences that have a certain, deeper, and perhaps even powerful meaning for yourself, for your Self.

This is quasi a written form of the so-called "mantra meditation," as described for example in the meditation booklet by Christopher Klein and Jens Helbig already mentioned before. It is about using words or sentences to calm and focus the mind by directing the mind to meanings that are actually meaningful for ourselves, for our Self.

As to myself, I started my calligraphy practice with the three characters of my Chinese name "吴 礼 贤", i.e., "Wú Lǐxián," which is a transcription—or better transliteration—of my last name "Ulrich" into Chinese characters, which—pronounced in Chinese—sounds quite similar to the name "Ulrich." This Chinese name "吴 礼 贤" has the meaning of "Mr. Wu, the courteous able and virtuous person." At the beginning of the book, I explained how that name was given to me and how it made me proud to receive such a name, its characters intended to reflect my Character (at least I try my best to show being worthy to bear this name).

You can see some early results of my calligraphy practice in this section in Fig. 12.6, written with a brush pen that I bought in Asia, the tip of the pen being similar to a small brush. Asian readers may forgive me the probably clumsy writing of the characters. I am aware that this too is a task for life, to learn and practice until being old of age, in the sense of the calligraphy Huó dào lǎo, xué dào lǎo 活到老, 学到老 at the beginning of this book.

Thus by practicing the art of calligraphy, focusing on the lines of the characters of my Chinese name, observing my breathing and posture, focusing on it, and trying to let my thoughts go, I actually focus on myself, on Mindfulness, and inner Centricity of the mind.

Religious Mindfulness

We should not forget that, besides Asian forms of mediation techniques and meditation practice, certain forms of meditative or contemplative practice have also existed in other cultures for a long time (Fig. 12.7). I would particularly like to go into the practice of religious prayer and religious contemplation, that is, religious Mindfulness. Many religions use religious images and symbols to clarify what they stand for, what the essence, the Character of the religion is. You will surely remember the chapter from the beginning of this book "Via Character to Centricity," in which I suggested to choose a totem as a symbol for your Character. On the other hand, I just introduced calligraphy as a possible way of meditative practice in the previous section. Interestingly, calligraphy can also be found in religious places, as spiritual contemplative elements, especially in Muslim mosques, as shown in Fig. 12.7.

We can find the practice of religious prayer and religious contemplation in many religions of the world, although of course practiced differently in every religion. You can experience this by yourself by taking the time to visit a religious place, no matter of which religion, be it a Christian church, a Muslim mosque, a Buddhist temple, or a Hindu temple, and you can "breathe the presence" of this religious Place and the believers gathered there. Even if you are not a believer in this particular religion, it may still happen, that you will feel something inside yourself:

- A calm that spreads in your mind
- An energy that fills your body from the inside
- A Focus directed to the essential, valuable Thoughts

Fig. 12.7 Religious prayer, religious contemplation, and religious Mindfulness (source: own photo)

– A growing understanding of what is truly important in your life

You may ask:

Why is that so?

Because religions have been dealing with the essential questions of mankind, of life, of our personal life for thousands of years. Religions have made it their mission to give us an answer to these essential questions, a way to deal with them. Especially to questions to which there are often no logical, scientific answers:

- Who am I?
- Where do I come from?
- Why am I here?
- Where will I go to when all this is over?

Of course, natural sciences are also looking for answers to these questions, and they have already produced astonishing things. For example, physics and astronomy have found a scientific explanation for the origin of the universe: the Big Bang theory: Biology and genetics have developed the theory of evolution as an explanation for the origin and development of life on earth. In addition, medical sciences provide explanations for the question why we are getting sick and for the (biological) death of human beings.

Interestingly—at least to my understanding—there is very little literature that deals with a connection between religion and management or Leadership, such as the book by Paul J. Kohtes "Jesus für Manager" (i.e., Jesus for Managers, Kohtes 2008). However, we see an increasing number of literature that builds a bridge between different spiritual directions. It is building on the underlying, common spiritual foundations, such as Ruben Habito's book "Living Zen, Loving God" (Habito 1995, German publication "Zen leben— Christ bleiben," Habito 2006).

In his book, Ruben Habito very clearly describes the connections and similarities between Zen spirituality—i.e., spirituality in the sense of meditation—and religious, Christian spirituality. As Habito explains, spirituality (lat spiritus) in Christian understanding has a meaning of "breath of God" and thus for a life in harmony with God, with the breath of God and of harmony with the mind and Spirit. We have already seen in previous sections of this book that breath is the essential basis of essentially any Asian practice, art, or meditation technique. Being in harmony with the mind is understood as Mindfulness in meditation practice.

Yet the essential questions remain:

- Who am I?
- Where do I come from?
- Why am I here?
- Where will I go to when all this is over?

In fact, in this book we have already dealt extensively with the question of "Who am I" on the different levels of the concept of Spiritual Leadership as well as with their importance for Centricity, for inner Centricity. If you are looking for answers to the other essential questions, then the path of religion may be a suitable way for you to find help, a way, a spiritual way for your life. Far be it from me to do missionary work, to convert you to religion, or even to any specific religion. As I said at the beginning:

> This book is not a religious book.

Now you can ask yourself: What does Leadership have to do with religious spirituality—even if it is understood as a Spiritual Leadership?

The answer is: We should understand and recognize as Leaders, that for each of, us the respective religion of our own culture—and increasingly also religions of other cultures—have shaped us, ourselves, our Self, and our environment, whether we want it or not. The Character, our culture, our Habits, what we do, our Words, our Thoughts, and our Values have been shaped by it. It is what generally makes up our spiritual interior. Therefore, we can ask ourselves again how we can become aware of what shaped us in a spiritual sense, focus on it and recognize our inner spiritual core in order to strengthen our inner Centricity.

You can use appropriate spiritual practices, contemplations, prayers, and of course religious, spiritual objects to support this spiritual knowledge. Remember the "reminders" that I recommended in Chap. 10. Many religions know such types of "reminders" as spiritual objects for prayer or contemplation, such as in the form of prayer beads (Fig. 12.8). Be it a Christian rosary,

Fig. 12.8 Spiritual practice in religion (source: http://www.pixabay.com, created by Myriam-Fotos, amended)

a Buddhist prayer beads, or an Islamic Tasbih prayer beads. All of these practices, contemplations, prayers, and spiritual objects can help you focus your
mind and increase your personal inner Centricity.

Conclusion for Your Leadership

Why should we—as Leaders—consider working on inner Centricity? Because
we are all living in a much more dynamic environment today, working on
multiple tasks at the same time and are often so busy with all kinds of things
that we forget to take a moment to just lean back, close our eyes, and just
breathe. In addition, to draw energy from ourselves, from our Self, from
within, an energy that truly helps us to develop a strong, authentic, and even
spiritual Leadership.

A character, a mind, and a soul with a calm and stable inner Centricity will
naturally develop an overlying level of positive and strong core Values such as
respect, fairness, honesty, and reliability. The inner energy source that drives
these core Values, the inner Centricity, remains unchanged and stable, like the
trunk of a tree, and forms the "center of gravity" of your Character, your
mind, and your soul.

Meditation and meditative techniques help us and lead us to freeing our
own mind. Through clarity and Focus of the mind, through Mindfulness, one
can achieve an inner Centricity, which also materializes as Focus and Centricity
on the outer levels of the Spiritual Leadership concept, and which can be
perceived by others as Focus and Centricity of Values, Thoughts, Words,
and Action.

We should also be aware that, besides Asian forms of mediation techniques
and meditation practice, certain forms of meditative or contemplative practice also exist in other cultures and religions, such as religious prayers and
religious contemplation, i.e., religious Mindfulness. As Leaders, we should
understand and recognize that, for each of us, also the respective religion of
our culture has shaped us, ourselves, our Self, and our environment, whether
we want it or not. The Character, our culture, our Habits, what we do, our
Words, our Thoughts, and our Values have been shaped by it. It is what generally makes up our spiritual interior. So we can ask ourselves how—in return—
we can become aware of what shaped us in a spiritual sense, focus on it and
recognize our inner spiritual core in order to strengthen our inner Centricity.

References

Chozuan S, Tengu-Geijutsu-Ron – Diskurs über die Kunst der Bergdämonen (über das wahre Prinzip der Schwertkunst, 1728, e.g. in Kammer R (1993) ZEN in der Kunst, das Schwert zu führen, O.W. Barth Verlag, Frankfurt a.M

Davey HE (1999) Brush meditation. Stone Bridge Press, Berkeley

Dürckheim K (2012) Hara, O.W. Barth, Frankfurt a.M.

Fontana D (1999) The meditation handbook: the practical guide to eastern and western meditation techniques. Watkins Publishing, London

Gamsjäger T (2016) Meditation für Anfänger. CreateSpace, North Charleston

Geshe KB (2013) The new meditation handbook. Tharpa Publications, Ulverston

Habito R (1995) Living Zen. Wisdom Publications, Boston, Loving God

Habito R (2006) Zen leben – Christ bleiben. O.W. Barth, Frankfurt a.M.

Herriegel E (1958) Der Zen-Weg. O.W. Barth, Frankfurt a.M

Herriegel E (1989) Zen in the art of archery. Vintage Random House, New York

Herriegel E (1999) Zen in der Kunst des Bogenschießens. O.W. Barth, Frankfurt a.M

Klein C, Helbig J (2017) Meditation für Anfänger. GbR, Düsseldorf

Kohtes PJ (2008) Jesus für Manager – Frei sein im Job und im Leben. J Kamphausen Verlag

Lehrhaupt L (2013) T'ai Chi as a path of wisdom. Shambala Publications, Boston

Mills E (2017) Inhale – Exhale – repeat: a meditation handbook for every part of your day. Rider Books, London

Pater R (1988) LEADING from WITHIN. Park Street Press, Rochester

Schloegel I (1995) Was ist Zen. O.W. Barth, Frankfurt a.M.

Suzuki S (1975) Zen-Geist – Anfänger-Geist. Theseus, Zürich

Suzuki S (2006) Zen Mind – Beginner's Mind. Shambhala, Boston

Zabel RM (2013) Meditation. It's not what you think. Mel Zabel – Awareness Exercises – AmTrade LLC, Los Angeles

13

Epilogue: Some Further Thoughts at the End

At the end of this book, I would like to share a few thoughts with you that go beyond the concept of Spiritual Leadership and Centricity, thoughts from my personal experience of Leadership that could be helpful for your own Leadership.

Dare to Take Risks and to Fail!

In the harbor, a ship is safe,
    however, that is not what it was built for.
    (Seneca)

Mistakes and failures are part of every learning process, part of Leadership and of every decision-making; they are part of our lives. Trying to avoid failure means trying to avoid the reality of our lives. Dealing actively with mistakes and failures means active and true Leadership. On the other hand, fear of mistakes, fear of failure leads to fear of decisions.

This fear of mistakes, of failure comes from our—western—desire and habit to control the results of our Actions and to measure them against targets, KPIs, and business successes, where everything that "goes wrong" is considered as a failure. Nowadays, however, Leaders have to deal with complex situations and/or people. The new "buzzword" VUCA is supposed to describe such a situation, as it stands for "Volatility, Uncertainty, Complexity,

T. H. Ulrich, *Spiritual Leadership*, https://doi.org/10.1007/978-3-030-45432-6_13

and Ambiguity." This is actually nothing new, because every nontrivial situation always contains a certain degree of "volatility, uncertainty, complexity, and ambiguity," and always has been. Is it not true that, e.g., Christopher Columbus was constantly confronted with "Volatility, Uncertainty, Complexity, and Ambiguity" on his journey toward the discovery of America (to pick up the analogy of the ship again)? After all, he in fact had set out to find a sea route to India westward, so he clearly was mistaken and his mission clearly had failed. Nowadays, we understand that his "mistake" and failure have in fact opened up a full continent, a new world.

As Leaders, we need to develop an understanding that we cannot plan and control everything. That we have to accept that good Leadership will always involve risks that can lead to both: success, or mistakes and failures.

Let us once again have a look at a group of people who regularly have to deal with VUCA situations, with Leadership, decision-making and mistakes/failures, and who are even regularly criticized for this in the media. Yet they do their job with full commitment: I am talking about referees.

The already mentioned world-class football (US: soccer) referee Urs Meier describes in his book "Du bist die Entscheidung" that fear as such is not bad in itself, if it is understood as a source of additional information instead of a mechanism for self-blocking (Meier 2010). Urs Meier also emphasizes that a fear of taking a decision, with the consequence not to take any decision, is nevertheless also a decision. Namely, the decision not to take a decision. Therefore, no matter how we act, in any case there are effects and impacts, based on a decision taken with respect to a certain issue, or on the fact that you decide to not decide the issue.

According to my personal experience in business life, there is always a remaining risk in many situations in today's Leadership and management environment. The risk of failing in processes, the risk of failing in decisions, the risk of failing in front of customers, and much more. These risks are increasing: the less defined the framework conditions are in a certain business environment, the less certain the requirements, parameters, and objectives which we as a Leader are confronted with. In other words, the more we are in a typical VUCA situation.

To visualize dependencies for typical risk situations, I developed for myself—and for the visualization toward top management—the empirical (qualitative) risk management dependency curve as shown in Fig. 13.1, which depicts the relationship between effort/expenditure and remaining risk.

Here is a brief explanation of what this risk management dependency curve means:

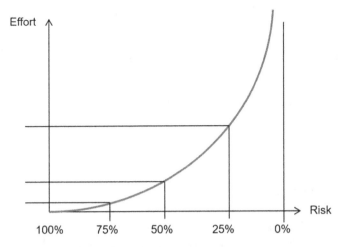

Fig. 13.1 Risk dependencies

1. There is never "zero risk," because one would have to spend an infinite amount of effort/expenditure to achieve this "zero risk" state.
2. If you do not make any effort/expenses, you can be sure that you take the full risk, i.e., 100% risk.
3. The difficult part of it:

   – In the area of low effort/expendiclarge lever of risk reduction can be achieved with a bit more effort/expenditure through active risk management.
   – However, the more effort you put into active risk management, the more difficult it becomes and the more it costs to further reduce the remaining risk significantly.

4. Here is the point where you, as Leader and manager, come into play and have to make active decisions. Therefore, you have to decide whether the remaining risk is acceptable for you as a Leader and manager, or whether you want to further reduce the remaining risk, and what additional effort you consider reasonable under entrepreneurial criteria.
5. However, no matter how much effort/expenditure you bring in: there is always a remaining, residual risk; there is always the risk of failure. You cannot avoid it, no matter what you do!

The good news is:

The more our environment develops in the direction of the VUCA situation, the more our Leadership is in demand, the more *WE* are required as Leaders to step in, to lead and to guide.

Therefore:

> Risks are a source for true success.

As we can learn from a first historic quote:

What would life be
if we would not have the courage
to risk something.
(Vincent van Gogh)

It is like in the stock market: the big wins can only be achieved in those investments in which lie the biggest risks. If you choose a safe form of investment, you will generate predictable but also very modest profits. To put it briefly: no one has ever got rich with a passbook as financial investment. Only those who dare to leave their comfort zone, who dare to take a risk, and who dare to fail, have the chance to develop further, as many wise and globally experienced characters already pointed out:

Success means
to stand up one time more
than you fell.
(Winston Churchill)

The same wisdom is common in the martial arts that we already heard of in Chap. 8:

Karate is seven times falling down
and eight times standing up again.

However, this book is not so much about how to become particularly successful in business. It is more about ourselves, about our spiritual Self. Why should ventures, risks, and failures be significant for our spiritual Self, significant for what and how we are?

A physically handicapped friend whom I got to know in France during my studies abroad once said a very important sentence that had a great impact on me:

Pour savoir être heureux,
il faut d'abord connaître la tristesse.
(To know how to be happy,
You must first know sadness)

Venture/risk and happiness/joy are two sides of the same coin. Those who dare to take risks, who have experienced failure, but do not let themselves be discouraged by it, rather incorporate the possibility and Awareness of failure into the risks that they take, those have the prospect to experience, to live real joy and happiness.

In his book "Meditation… It is not what you think" (Zabel 2013), Mel Zabel describes that we often—far too often—look for joy and happiness in material things, in objects, rather than in inner Values: in money, power, status, status symbols, shopping orgies, delusions of beauty and other things and behaviors that the modern consumer industry and consumer society wants us to believe in, as the feigned source of infinite happiness. However, just as often, we fail. Because the source of true joy and happiness can rather be found in immaterial things, in situations in which we risk something, leave our comfort zone, are brave and accept failure as a natural part of the risk and venture.

Take as example the cries of joy that someone cries out from the bottom of his heart, from his very core after having jumped off a bridge with bungee rope at his feet. Other example is the infinite joy when a nearly defeated team rears up again, takes full risk and gains a victory in the last minutes of a match that everybody already believed lost.

In German football history, there was such a match that I personally remember well, as it took place on the day of my 33rd birthday: it was the decisive match of the German football championship of May 19, 2001. Bayern Munich played against the Hamburg team HSV, being nearly defeated 0:1 during the regular match time of 90 min. The direct championship competitor in the German premier league, the team of Schalke 04, already believed to be the winner and champion of the season after winning their respective last match in the same minute. Still, in a little bit of overtime allowed by the referee, Bayern München scored a goal taking full risk with one last brave and powerful shot, equalized to 1:1, and got the necessary extra point to win the championship in a big roar. I assume my non-German readers may not be familiar with this special match from German football history; however, I am convinced that everyone has experienced such kind of goosebumps moments in his life.

Doing and Not Doing

Maybe you now have the impression that this book is actually about "doing nothing," but rather just sitting around, meditating, and trying to find a glimpse of inner Centricity. I understand that, in a culture in which we are measured based on targets and results, i.e., actions, this may appear strange. That doing nothing, "Not Doing" would be inappropriate and completely absurd for a manager, a Leader.

In a different culture, however, it is not strange at all. Daoism in China, for example, has known the already mentioned principle of Wu Wei (wúwéi 無為/无为), the principle of conscious "Not Doing" from the Tao Te King by Lao Tsu (Lǎozǐ 老子, Dàodéjīng 道德 经, Tzu 1999) since the sixth century BC. Bernhard Moestl also explains this principle in great detail in his book "Denken wie ein Shaolin—Die sieben Prinzipien emotionaler Selbstbestimmung" (Moestl 2016).

Wu Wei does not mean that you do not do anything, i.e., the absence of any consciousness or of any conscious Being. It rather means that you do something by consciously Not Doing, by consciously not intervening, by letting things develop out of themselves (see also the book of Diana Renner and Steven D'Souza "Not Doing: The art of effortless action" (Renner and D'Souza 2018)).

As already mentioned, Urs Meier also describes in his book "Du bist die Entscheidung" (Meier 2010), that a non-decision is also a decision, namely a decision for not taking a decision on a certain issue. In fact, that is a form of the Daoist Wu Wei, namely doing through active, conscious Not Doing.

As Leaders, we need to develop an understanding that we cannot always do "something." That we cannot only measure ourselves by what we do, but also by what we consciously do not do, our Not Doing. That we also have to accept that both our doing and our Not Doing always involve imponderables and risks, which, however, are an opportunity for us to grow continuously and to develop further, whether they lead to success, mistakes, or failure. However, what helps us to keep an orientation, a direction, so that our Leadership does not become "arbitrary" in situations in which we are increasingly faced with uncertainties and increasingly have to take risks? It is the Centricity described in this book, and the understanding how it materializes on the different levels of Spiritual Leadership, that give us the stability not to "tumble," even in VUCA situations.

Conclusion for Your Leadership

As Leaders have to develop an understanding that we cannot plan and control everything. It means to accept that living good Leadership will always involve taking risks, which can lead to both: either success, or mistakes and failures. Venture/risk and happiness/joy are two sides of the same coin. If you dare to take risks and to experience failure, however if you do not let yourself be discouraged by it, rather incorporate the possibility and Awareness of failure into the risks that you take, then you have the prospect to experience, to live real joy and happiness.

On the other hand, we have to develop an Awareness that we cannot always "do something." That we should not only measure our success and ourselves by what we *do*, but also by what we *consciously* do *not* do. In China this principle is called Wu Wei (wúwéi 無為/无为). We also have to accept that both, our doing and our Not Doing, always involve imponderables and risks, which, however, are an opportunity for us to grow further and to develop ourselves further, no matter if they lead to success, mistakes, or failure.

References

Lao Tzu (Lǎozǐ 老子), Tao Te King (Dàodéjīng 道德经), 6th. Century B.C., e.g.. in Wing, R.L., (1999) Der Weg und die Kraft, Tao-te-king, Bechtermünz, Augsburg

Meier U (2010) Du bist die Entscheidung – schnell und entschlossen handeln. Fischer Taschenbuch, Frankfurt a.M

Moestl B (2016) Denken wie ein Shaolin – Die sieben Prinzipien emotionaler Selbstbestimmung. Knaur, München

Renner D, D'Souza S (2018) Not Doing: The art of effortless action. LID Publishing, London

Zabel RM (2013) Meditation. It's not what you think. Mel Zabel – Awareness Exercises – AmTrade LLC, Los Angeles